Dear reader,

thank you for your trust and for buying this book. I'm always glad to see someone with a desire to get closer to God, to accept Him as their Lord and Saviour and invite Him into their everyday life, to each and every part of it.

By studying His Word systematically, each and every day is a day we live with Him, we let Him illuminate the path of our lives.

I am glad that together we can walk this wonderful path. I ask each of you to pray for me, and I, for my part, promise to remember each and every one of you in my prayers.

Before every encounter with the Lord in His Word, let us pray to the Holy Spirit, may He guide us, for He is the true author of this Word and, at the same time, He knows us better than anyone else, better even than we know ourselves. May He speak directly to our hearts, our minds. May He enter with His Word into our lives, into all our affairs - the pleasant ones as well as the difficult ones

After praying to the Holy Spirit, let us read a given passage of the Scripture. Let's do this slowly, we may even repeat it several times. The Lord will speak to us sometimes through a whole passage, sometimes through a single sentence or word. Sometimes He speaks immediately, sometimes He speaks subtly, after a long time.

Let's write down what the Lord wants to say through the given passage. His Word will sustain us as we remember it throughout the day, act and live with it, with HIM.

May The Lord in Heaven bless you, dear reader. Amen.

CONTENTS

Principal celebrations of the liturgical year 2024, Cycles — lectionary for mass 3
January 4-13
February 13-24
March 24-62
April 62-70
May 70-78
June 78-89
July 89-97
August 97-108
September 108-119
October 119-127
November 127-137
December 137-154

PRINCIPAL CELEBRATIONS OF THE LITURGICAL YEAR 2024

First Sunday of Advent	December 3, 2023
Ash Wednesday	February 14, 2024
Easter Sunday	March 31, 2024
The Ascension of the Lord [Thursday]	May 9, 2024
Pentecost Sunday	May 19, 2024
The Most Holy Body and Blood of Christ	June 2, 2024
First Sunday of Advent	December 1, 2024

CYCLES — LECTIONARY FOR MASS

Sunday Cycle	YEAR B	December 3, 2023 to November 24, 2024
Weekday Cycle	CYCLE II	January 9 to February 13, 2024 May 20 to November 30, 2024
Sunday Cycle	YEAR C	December 1, 2024 to November 23, 2025

Monday, January 1, 2024
SOLEMNITY OF MARY, THE HOLY MOTHER OF GOD

First Reading: Numbers 6: 22-27

22 Yahweh spoke to Moses, saying, 23 "Speak to Aaron and to his sons, saying, 'This is how you shall bless the children of Israel.' You shall tell them, 24 'Yahweh bless you, and keep you. 25 Yahweh make his face to shine on you, and be gracious to you. 26 Yahweh lift up his face toward you, and give you peace.' 27 "So they shall put my name on the children of Israel; and I will bless them."

Responsorial Psalm: Psalms 67: 2-3, 5, 6, 8

2 That your way may be known on earth,
and your salvation among all nations,
3 let the peoples praise you, God.
Let all the peoples praise you.
5 Let the peoples praise you, God.
Let all the peoples praise you.
6 The earth has yielded its increase.
God, even our own God, will bless us.
8 God will bless us.
All the ends of the earth shall fear him.

Second Reading: Galatians 4: 4-7

4 But when the fullness of the time came, God sent out his Son, born to a woman, born under the law, 5 that he might redeem those who were under the law, that we might receive the adoption as children. 6 And because you are children, God sent out the Spirit of his Son into your hearts, crying, "Abba,† Father!" 7 So you are no longer a bondservant, but a son; and if a son, then an heir of God through Christ.

Gospel: Luke 2: 16-21

16 They came with haste and found both Mary and Joseph, and the baby was lying in the feeding trough. 17 When they saw it, they publicized widely the saying which was spoken to them about this child. 18 All who heard it wondered at the things which were spoken to them by the shepherds. 19 But Mary kept all these sayings, pondering them in her heart.
20 The shepherds returned, glorifying and praising God for all the things that they had heard and seen, just as it was told them. 21 When eight days were fulfilled for the circumcision of the child, his name was called Jesus, which was given by the angel before he was conceived in the womb.

1. Invite the Holy Spirit into this reading, asking the Author of Scripture to speak to you through His Word
2. Read today's passage as many times as you need, take your time
3. Write down (below) what the Lord is saying to you today
4. Live with this Word in your heart through the day

_____

_____

Sunday, January 7, 2024
Epiphany of the Lord Solemnity

First Reading: Isaiah 60: 1-6

1 "Arise, shine; for your light has come, and Yahweh's glory has risen on you!
2 For behold, darkness will cover the earth, and thick darkness the peoples;
but Yahweh will arise on you, and his glory shall be seen on you.
3 Nations will come to your light, and kings to the brightness of your rising.
4 "Lift up your eyes all around, and see: they all gather themselves together.
They come to you. Your sons will come from far away, and your daughters will be carried in arms.
5 Then you shall see and be radiant, and your heart will thrill and be enlarged;
because the abundance of the sea will be turned to you. The wealth of the nations will come to you.
6 A multitude of camels will cover you, the dromedaries of Midian and Ephah.

All from Sheba will come. They will bring gold and frankincense,
and will proclaim the praises of Yahweh.

Responsorial Psalm: Psalms 72: 1-2, 7-8, 10-13

1 God, give the king your justice;
your righteousness to the royal son.
2 He will judge your people with righteousness,
and your poor with justice.
7 In his days, the righteous shall flourish,
and abundance of peace, until the moon is no more.
8 He shall have dominion also from sea to sea,
from the River to the ends of the earth.
10 The kings of Tarshish and of the islands will bring tribute.
The kings of Sheba and Seba shall offer gifts.
11 Yes, all kings shall fall down before him.
All nations shall serve him.
12 For he will deliver the needy when he cries;
the poor, who has no helper.
13 He will have pity on the poor and needy.
He will save the souls of the needy.

Second Reading: Ephesians 3: 2-3a, 5-6

2 if it is so that you have heard of the administration of that grace of God which was given me toward you, 3 how that by revelation the mystery was made known to me, 5 which in other generations was not made known to the children of men, as it has now been revealed to his holy apostles and prophets in the Spirit, 6 that the Gentiles are fellow heirs and fellow members of the body, and fellow partakers of his promise in Christ Jesus through the Good News

Gospel: Matthew 2: 1-12

1 Now when Jesus was born in Bethlehem of Judea in the days of King Herod, behold, wise men† from the east came to Jerusalem, saying, 2 "Where is he who is born King

of the Jews? For we saw his star in the east, and have come to worship him." 3 When King Herod heard it, he was troubled, and all Jerusalem with him. 4 Gathering together all the chief priests and scribes of the people, he asked them where the Christ would be born. 5 They said to him, "In Bethlehem of Judea, for this is written through the prophet,

6 'You Bethlehem, land of Judah,
are in no way least among the princes of Judah;
for out of you shall come a governor
who shall shepherd my people, Israel.' "*

7 Then Herod secretly called the wise men, and learned from them exactly what time the star appeared. 8 He sent them to Bethlehem, and said, "Go and search diligently for the young child. When you have found him, bring me word, so that I also may come and worship him."

9 They, having heard the king, went their way; and behold, the star, which they saw in the east, went before them until it came and stood over where the young child was. 10 When they saw the star, they rejoiced with exceedingly great joy. 11 They came into the house and saw the young child with Mary, his mother, and they fell down and worshiped him. Opening their treasures, they offered to him gifts: gold, frankincense, and myrrh. 12 Being warned in a dream not to return to Herod, they went back to their own country another way.

1. Invite the Holy Spirit into this reading, asking the Author of Scripture to speak to you through His Word
2. Read today's passage as many times as you need, take your time
3. Write down (below) what the Lord is saying to you today
4. Live with this Word in your heart through the day

_____

_____

Sunday, January 14, 2024
Second Sunday in Ordinary Time

First Reading: First Samuel 3: 3b-10, 19

3 and God's lamp hadn't yet gone out, and Samuel had laid down in Yahweh's temple where God's ark was, 4 Yahweh called Samuel. He said, "Here I am."
5 He ran to Eli and said, "Here I am; for you called me."
He said, "I didn't call. Lie down again."
He went and lay down. 6 Yahweh called yet again, "Samuel!"
Samuel arose and went to Eli and said, "Here I am; for you called me."
He answered, "I didn't call, my son. Lie down again." 7 Now Samuel didn't yet know Yahweh, neither was Yahweh's word yet revealed to him. 8 Yahweh called Samuel again the third time. He arose and went to Eli and said, "Here I am; for you called me."
Eli perceived that Yahweh had called the child. 9 Therefore Eli said to Samuel, "Go, lie down. It shall be, if he calls you, that you shall say, 'Speak, Yahweh; for your servant hears.' " So Samuel went and lay down in his place. 10 Yahweh came, and stood, and called as at other times, "Samuel! Samuel!"
Then Samuel said, "Speak; for your servant hears."
19 Samuel grew, and Yahweh was with him and let none of his words fall to the ground.

Responsorial Psalm: Psalms 40: 2, 4ab, 7-10

2 He brought me up also out of a horrible pit,
out of the miry clay.
He set my feet on a rock,
and gave me a firm place to stand.
3 He has put a new song in my mouth, even praise to our God.
Many shall see it, and fear, and shall trust in Yahweh.
4 Blessed is the man who makes Yahweh his trust,
and doesn't respect the proud, nor such as turn away to lies.
7 Then I said, "Behold, I have come.
It is written about me in the book in the scroll.
8 I delight to do your will, my God.
Yes, your law is within my heart."
9 I have proclaimed glad news of righteousness in the great assembly.
Behold, I will not seal my lips, Yahweh, you know.
10 I have not hidden your righteousness within my heart.
I have declared your faithfulness and your salvation.
I have not concealed your loving kindness and your truth from the great assembly.

Second Reading: First Corinthians 6: 13c-15a, 17-20

13 But the body is not for sexual immorality, but for the Lord, and the Lord for the body. 14 Now God raised up the Lord, and will also raise us up by his power. 15 Don't you know that your bodies are members of Christ?
17 But he who is joined to the Lord is one spirit. 18 Flee sexual immorality! "Every sin that a man does is outside the body," but he who commits sexual immorality sins against his own body. 19 Or don't you know that your body is a temple of the Holy Spirit who is in you, whom you have from God? You are not your own, 20 for you were bought with a price. Therefore glorify God in your body and in your spirit, which are God's.

Gospel: John 1: 35-42

35 Again, the next day, John was standing with two of his disciples, 36 and he looked at Jesus as he walked, and said, "Behold, the Lamb of God!" 37 The two disciples heard him speak, and they followed Jesus. 38 Jesus turned and saw them following, and said to them, "What are you looking for?"
They said to him, "Rabbi" (which is to say, being interpreted, Teacher), "where are you staying?"
39 He said to them, "Come and see."
They came and saw where he was staying, and they stayed with him that day. It was about the tenth hour.† 40 One of the two who heard John and followed him was Andrew, Simon Peter's brother. 41 He first found his own brother, Simon, and said to him, "We have found the Messiah!" (which is, being interpreted, Christ‡). 42 He brought him to Jesus. Jesus looked at him and said, "You are Simon the son of Jonah. You shall be called Cephas" (which is by interpretation, Peter).

1. Invite the Holy Spirit into this reading, asking the Author of Scripture to speak to you through His Word
2. Read today's passage as many times as you need, take your time
3. Write down (below) what the Lord is saying to you today
4. Live with this Word in your heart through the day

_____

_____

Sunday, January 21, 2024
Third Sunday in Ordinary Time

First Reading: Jonah 3: 1-5, 10

1 Yahweh's word came to Jonah the second time, saying, 2 "Arise, go to Nineveh, that great city, and preach to it the message that I give you."
3 So Jonah arose, and went to Nineveh, according to Yahweh's word. Now Nineveh was an exceedingly great city, three days' journey across. 4 Jonah began to enter into the city a day's journey, and he cried out, and said, "In forty days, Nineveh will be overthrown!"
5 The people of Nineveh believed God; and they proclaimed a fast and put on sackcloth, from their greatest even to their least.
10 God saw their works, that they turned from their evil way. God relented of the disaster which he said he would do to them, and he didn't do it.

Responsorial Psalm: Psalms 25: 4-9

4 Show me your ways, Yahweh.
Teach me your paths.
5 Guide me in your truth, and teach me,
for you are the God of my salvation.
I wait for you all day long.
6 Yahweh, remember your tender mercies and your loving kindness,
for they are from old times.
7 Don't remember the sins of my youth, nor my transgressions.
Remember me according to your loving kindness,
for your goodness' sake, Yahweh.
8 Good and upright is Yahweh,
therefore he will instruct sinners in the way.
9 He will guide the humble in justice.
He will teach the humble his way.

Second Reading: First Corinthians 7: 29-31

29 But I say this, brothers: the time is short. From now on, both those who have wives may be as though they had none; 30 and those who weep, as though they didn't weep; and those who rejoice, as though they didn't rejoice; and those who buy, as though they didn't possess; 31 and those who use the world, as not using it to the fullest. For the mode of this world passes away.

Gospel: Mark 1: 14-20

14 Now after John was taken into custody, Jesus came into Galilee, preaching the Good News of God's Kingdom, 15 and saying, "The time is fulfilled, and God's Kingdom is at hand! Repent, and believe in the Good News."
16 Passing along by the sea of Galilee, he saw Simon and Andrew, the brother of Simon, casting a net into the sea, for they were fishermen. 17 Jesus said to them, "Come after me, and I will make you into fishers for men."
18 Immediately they left their nets, and followed him.
19 Going on a little further from there, he saw James the son of Zebedee, and John his brother, who were also in the boat mending the nets. 20 Immediately he called them, and they left their father, Zebedee, in the boat with the hired servants, and went after him.

1. Invite the Holy Spirit into this reading, asking the Author of Scripture to speak to you through His Word
2. Read today's passage as many times as you need, take your time
3. Write down (below) what the Lord is saying to you today
4. Live with this Word in your heart through the day

_____

_____

Sunday, January 28, 2024
Fourth Sunday in Ordinary Time

First Reading: Deuteronomy 18: 15-20

15 Yahweh your God will raise up to you a prophet from among you, of your brothers, like me. You shall listen to him. 16 This is according to all that you desired of Yahweh your God in Horeb in the day of the assembly, saying, "Let me not hear again Yahweh my God's voice, neither let me see this great fire any more, that I not die."

17 Yahweh said to me, "They have well said that which they have spoken. 18 I will raise them up a prophet from among their brothers, like you. I will put my words in his mouth, and he shall speak to them all that I shall command him. 19 It shall happen, that whoever will not listen to my words which he shall speak in my name, I will require it of him. 20 But the prophet who speaks a word presumptuously in my name, which I have not commanded him to speak, or who speaks in the name of other gods, that same prophet shall die."

Responsorial Psalm: Psalms 95: 1-2, 6-9

1 Oh come, let's sing to Yahweh.
Let's shout aloud to the rock of our salvation!
2 Let's come before his presence with thanksgiving.
Let's extol him with songs!
6 Oh come, let's worship and bow down.
Let's kneel before Yahweh, our Maker,
7 for he is our God.
We are the people of his pasture,
and the sheep in his care.
Today, oh that you would hear his voice!
8 Don't harden your heart, as at Meribah,
as in the day of Massah in the wilderness,
9 when your fathers tempted me,
tested me, and saw my work.

Second Reading: First Corinthians 7: 32-35

32 But I desire to have you to be free from cares. He who is unmarried is concerned for the things of the Lord, how he may please the Lord; 33 but he who is married is concerned about the things of the world, how he may please his wife. 34 There is also a difference between a wife and a virgin. The unmarried woman cares about the things of the Lord, that she may be holy both in body and in spirit. But she who is married

cares about the things of the world—how she may please her husband. 35 This I say for your own benefit, not that I may ensnare you, but for that which is appropriate, and that you may attend to the Lord without distraction.

Gospel: Mark 1: 21-28

21 They went into Capernaum, and immediately on the Sabbath day he entered into the synagogue and taught. 22 They were astonished at his teaching, for he taught them as having authority, and not as the scribes. 23 Immediately there was in their synagogue a man with an unclean spirit, and he cried out, 24 saying, "Ha! What do we have to do with you, Jesus, you Nazarene? Have you come to destroy us? I know who you are: the Holy One of God!"
25 Jesus rebuked him, saying, "Be quiet, and come out of him!"
26 The unclean spirit, convulsing him and crying with a loud voice, came out of him. 27 They were all amazed, so that they questioned among themselves, saying, "What is this? A new teaching? For with authority he commands even the unclean spirits, and they obey him!" 28 The report of him went out immediately everywhere into all the region of Galilee and its surrounding area.

1. Invite the Holy Spirit into this reading, asking the Author of Scripture to speak to you through His Word
2. Read today's passage as many times as you need, take your time
3. Write down (below) what the Lord is saying to you today
4. Live with this Word in your heart through the day

_____

_____

Sunday, February 4, 2024
Fifth Sunday in Ordinary Time

First Reading: Job 7: 1-4, 6-7

1 "Isn't a man forced to labor on earth?

Aren't his days like the days of a hired hand?
2 As a servant who earnestly desires the shadow,
as a hireling who looks for his wages,
3 so I am made to possess months of misery,
wearisome nights are appointed to me.
4 When I lie down, I say,
'When will I arise, and the night be gone?'
I toss and turn until the dawning of the day.
6 My days are swifter than a weaver's shuttle,
and are spent without hope.
7 Oh remember that my life is a breath.
My eye will no more see good.

Responsorial Psalm: Psalms 147: 1-6

1 Praise Yah,
for it is good to sing praises to our God;
for it is pleasant and fitting to praise him.
2 Yahweh builds up Jerusalem.
He gathers together the outcasts of Israel.
3 He heals the broken in heart,
and binds up their wounds.
4 He counts the number of the stars.
He calls them all by their names.
5 Great is our Lord, and mighty in power.
His understanding is infinite.
6 Yahweh upholds the humble.
He brings the wicked down to the ground.

Second Reading: First Corinthians 9: 16-19, 22-23

16 For if I preach the Good News, I have nothing to boast about, for necessity is laid on me; but woe is to me if I don't preach the Good News. 17 For if I do this of my own will, I have a reward. But if not of my own will, I have a stewardship entrusted to me. 18 What then is my reward? That when I preach the Good News, I may present the Good News of Christ without charge, so as not to abuse my authority in the Good News.

19 For though I was free from all, I brought myself under bondage to all, that I might gain the more.
22 To the weak I became as weak, that I might gain the weak. I have become all things to all men, that I may by all means save some. 23 Now I do this for the sake of the Good News, that I may be a joint partaker of it.

Gospel: Mark 1: 29-39

29 Immediately, when they had come out of the synagogue, they came into the house of Simon and Andrew, with James and John. 30 Now Simon's wife's mother lay sick with a fever, and immediately they told him about her. 31 He came and took her by the hand and raised her up. The fever left her immediately,† and she served them.
32 At evening, when the sun had set, they brought to him all who were sick and those who were possessed by demons. 33 All the city was gathered together at the door. 34 He healed many who were sick with various diseases and cast out many demons. He didn't allow the demons to speak, because they knew him.
35 Early in the morning, while it was still dark, he rose up and went out, and departed into a deserted place, and prayed there. 36 Simon and those who were with him searched for him. 37 They found him and told him, "Everyone is looking for you."
38 He said to them, "Let's go elsewhere into the next towns, that I may preach there also, because I came out for this reason." 39 He went into their synagogues throughout all Galilee, preaching and casting out demons.

1. Invite the Holy Spirit into this reading, asking the Author of Scripture to speak to you through His Word
2. Read today's passage as many times as you need, take your time
3. Write down (below) what the Lord is saying to you today
4. Live with this Word in your heart through the day

_____
_____

Sunday, February 11, 2024
Sixth Sunday in Ordinary Time

First Reading: Leviticus 13: 1-2, 44-46

1 Yahweh spoke to Moses and to Aaron, saying, 2 "When a man shall have a swelling in his body's skin, or a scab, or a bright spot, and it becomes in the skin of his body the plague of leprosy, then he shall be brought to Aaron the priest or to one of his sons, the priests.
44 he is a leprous man. He is unclean. The priest shall surely pronounce him unclean. His plague is on his head.
45 "The leper in whom the plague is shall wear torn clothes, and the hair of his head shall hang loose. He shall cover his upper lip, and shall cry, 'Unclean! Unclean!' 46 All the days in which the plague is in him he shall be unclean. He is unclean. He shall dwell alone. His dwelling shall be outside of the camp.

Responsorial Psalm: Psalms 32: 1-2, 5, 11

1 Blessed is he whose disobedience is forgiven,
whose sin is covered.
2 Blessed is the man to whom Yahweh doesn't impute iniquity,
in whose spirit there is no deceit.
5 I acknowledged my sin to you.
I didn't hide my iniquity.
I said, I will confess my transgressions to Yahweh,
and you forgave the iniquity of my sin.
11 Be glad in Yahweh, and rejoice, you righteous!
Shout for joy, all you who are upright in heart!

Second Reading: First Corinthians 10: 31 – 11: 1

31 Whether therefore you eat or drink, or whatever you do, do all to the glory of God. 32 Give no occasion for stumbling, whether to Jews, to Greeks, or to the assembly of God; 33 even as I also please all men in all things, not seeking my own profit, but the profit of the many, that they may be saved.
1 Be imitators of me, even as I also am of Christ.

Gospel: Mark 1: 40-45

40 A leper came to him, begging him, kneeling down to him, and saying to him, "If you want to, you can make me clean."
41 Being moved with compassion, he stretched out his hand, and touched him, and said to him, "I want to. Be made clean." 42 When he had said this, immediately the leprosy departed from him and he was made clean. 43 He strictly warned him and immediately sent him out, 44 and said to him, "See that you say nothing to anybody, but go show yourself to the priest and offer for your cleansing the things which Moses commanded, for a testimony to them."
45 But he went out, and began to proclaim it much, and to spread about the matter, so that Jesus could no more openly enter into a city, but was outside in desert places. People came to him from everywhere.

1. Invite the Holy Spirit into this reading, asking the Author of Scripture to speak to you through His Word
2. Read today's passage as many times as you need, take your time
3. Write down (below) what the Lord is saying to you today
4. Live with this Word in your heart through the day

_____

_____

Wednesday, February 14, 2024
Ash Wednesday

First Reading: Joel 2: 12-18

12 "Yet even now," says Yahweh, "turn to me with all your heart,
and with fasting, and with weeping, and with mourning."
13 Tear your heart and not your garments,
and turn to Yahweh, your God;
for he is gracious and merciful,
slow to anger, and abundant in loving kindness,

and relents from sending calamity.
14 Who knows? He may turn and relent,
and leave a blessing behind him,
even a meal offering and a drink offering to Yahweh, your God.
15 Blow the trumpet in Zion!
Sanctify a fast.
Call a solemn assembly.
16 Gather the people.
Sanctify the assembly.
Assemble the elders.
Gather the children, and those who nurse from breasts.
Let the bridegroom go out of his room,
and the bride out of her chamber.
17 Let the priests, the ministers of Yahweh, weep between the porch and the altar,
and let them say, "Spare your people, Yahweh,
and don't give your heritage to reproach,
that the nations should rule over them.
Why should they say among the peoples,
'Where is their God?' "
18 Then Yahweh was jealous for his land,
and had pity on his people.

Responsorial Psalm: Psalms 51: 3-6, 12-14 and 17

3 For I know my transgressions.
My sin is constantly before me.
4 Against you, and you only, I have sinned,
and done that which is evil in your sight,
so you may be proved right when you speak,
and justified when you judge.
5 Behold, I was born in iniquity.
My mother conceived me in sin.
6 Behold, you desire truth in the inward parts.
You teach me wisdom in the inmost place.
12 Restore to me the joy of your salvation.
Uphold me with a willing spirit.
13 Then I will teach transgressors your ways.

Sinners will be converted to you.
14 Deliver me from the guilt of bloodshed, O God, the God of my salvation.
My tongue will sing aloud of your righteousness.
17 The sacrifices of God are a broken spirit.
O God, you will not despise a broken and contrite heart.

Second Reading: Second Corinthians 5: 20 – 6:2

20 We are therefore ambassadors on behalf of Christ, as though God were entreating by us: we beg you on behalf of Christ, be reconciled to God. 21 For him who knew no sin he made to be sin on our behalf, so that in him we might become the righteousness of God.
1 Working together, we entreat also that you do not receive the grace of God in vain. 2 For he says,
"At an acceptable time I listened to you.
In a day of salvation I helped you."*
Behold, now is the acceptable time. Behold, now is the day of salvation.

Gospel: Matthew 6: 1-6, 16-18

1 "Be careful that you don't do your charitable giving† before men, to be seen by them, or else you have no reward from your Father who is in heaven. 2 Therefore, when you do merciful deeds, don't sound a trumpet before yourself, as the hypocrites do in the synagogues and in the streets, that they may get glory from men. Most certainly I tell you, they have received their reward. 3 But when you do merciful deeds, don't let your left hand know what your right hand does, 4 so that your merciful deeds may be in secret, then your Father who sees in secret will reward you openly.
5 "When you pray, you shall not be as the hypocrites, for they love to stand and pray in the synagogues and in the corners of the streets, that they may be seen by men. Most certainly, I tell you, they have received their reward. 6 But you, when you pray, enter into your inner room, and having shut your door, pray to your Father who is in secret; and your Father who sees in secret will reward you openly.
16 "Moreover when you fast, don't be like the hypocrites, with sad faces. For they disfigure their faces that they may be seen by men to be fasting. Most certainly I tell you, they have received their reward. 17 But you, when you fast, anoint your head and

wash your face, 18 so that you are not seen by men to be fasting, but by your Father who is in secret; and your Father, who sees in secret, will reward you.

1. Invite the Holy Spirit into this reading, asking the Author of Scripture to speak to you through His Word
2. Read today's passage as many times as you need, take your time
3. Write down (below) what the Lord is saying to you today
4. Live with this Word in your heart through the day

_____

_____

Sunday, February 18, 2024
FIRST SUNDAY OF LENT

First Reading: Genesis 9: 8-15

8 God spoke to Noah and to his sons with him, saying, 9 "As for me, behold, I establish my covenant with you, and with your offspring after you, 10 and with every living creature that is with you: the birds, the livestock, and every animal of the earth with you, of all that go out of the ship, even every animal of the earth. 11 I will establish my covenant with you: All flesh will not be cut off any more by the waters of the flood. There will never again be a flood to destroy the earth." 12 God said, "This is the token of the covenant which I make between me and you and every living creature that is with you, for perpetual generations: 13 I set my rainbow in the cloud, and it will be a sign of a covenant between me and the earth. 14 When I bring a cloud over the earth, that the rainbow will be seen in the cloud, 15 I will remember my covenant, which is between me and you and every living creature of all flesh, and the waters will no more become a flood to destroy all flesh.

Responsorial Psalm: Psalms 25: 4-9

4 Show me your ways, Yahweh.
Teach me your paths.

5 Guide me in your truth, and teach me,
for you are the God of my salvation.
I wait for you all day long.
6 Yahweh, remember your tender mercies and your loving kindness,
for they are from old times.
7 Don't remember the sins of my youth, nor my transgressions.
Remember me according to your loving kindness,
for your goodness' sake, Yahweh.
8 Good and upright is Yahweh,
therefore he will instruct sinners in the way.
9 He will guide the humble in justice.
He will teach the humble his way.

Second Reading: First Peter 3: 18-22

18 Because Christ also suffered for sins once, the righteous for the unrighteous, that he might bring you to God, being put to death in the flesh, but made alive in the Spirit, 19 in whom he also went and preached to the spirits in prison, 20 who before were disobedient when God waited patiently in the days of Noah while the ship was being built. In it, few, that is, eight souls, were saved through water. 21 This is a symbol of baptism, which now saves you—not the putting away of the filth of the flesh, but the answer of a good conscience toward God—through the resurrection of Jesus Christ, 22 who is at the right hand of God, having gone into heaven, angels and authorities and powers being made subject to him.

Gospel: Mark 1: 12-15

12 Immediately the Spirit drove him out into the wilderness. 13 He was there in the wilderness forty days, tempted by Satan. He was with the wild animals; and the angels were serving him.
14 Now after John was taken into custody, Jesus came into Galilee, preaching the Good News of God's Kingdom, 15 and saying, "The time is fulfilled, and God's Kingdom is at hand! Repent, and believe in the Good News."

1. Invite the Holy Spirit into this reading, asking the Author of Scripture to speak to you through His Word

2. Read today's passage as many times as you need, take your time
3. Write down (below) what the Lord is saying to you today
4. Live with this Word in your heart through the day

_____

_____

Sunday, February 25, 2024
Second Sunday Of Lent

First Reading: Genesis 22: 1-2, 9a, 10-13, 15-18

1 After these things, God tested Abraham, and said to him, "Abraham!"
He said, "Here I am."
2 He said, "Now take your son, your only son, Isaac, whom you love, and go into the land of Moriah. Offer him there as a burnt offering on one of the mountains which I will tell you of."
9 They came to the place which God had told him of.
10 Abraham stretched out his hand, and took the knife to kill his son.
11 Yahweh's angel called to him out of the sky, and said, "Abraham, Abraham!"
He said, "Here I am."
12 He said, "Don't lay your hand on the boy or do anything to him. For now I know that you fear God, since you have not withheld your son, your only son, from me."
13 Abraham lifted up his eyes, and looked, and saw that behind him was a ram caught in the thicket by his horns. Abraham went and took the ram, and offered him up for a burnt offering instead of his son.
15 Yahweh's angel called to Abraham a second time out of the sky, 16 and said, " 'I have sworn by myself,' says Yahweh, 'because you have done this thing, and have not withheld your son, your only son, 17 that I will bless you greatly, and I will multiply your offspring greatly like the stars of the heavens, and like the sand which is on the seashore. Your offspring will possess the gate of his enemies. 18 All the nations of the earth will be blessed by your offspring, because you have obeyed my voice.' "

Responsorial Psalm: Psalms 116: 10, 15-19

10 I believed, therefore I said,

"I was greatly afflicted."
15 Precious in Yahweh's sight is the death of his saints.
16 Yahweh, truly I am your servant.
I am your servant, the son of your servant girl.
You have freed me from my chains.
17 I will offer to you the sacrifice of thanksgiving,
and will call on Yahweh's name.
18 I will pay my vows to Yahweh,
yes, in the presence of all his people,
19 in the courts of Yahweh's house,
in the middle of you, Jerusalem.
Praise Yah!

Second Reading: Romans 8: 31b-34

If God is for us, who can be against us? 32 He who didn't spare his own Son, but delivered him up for us all, how would he not also with him freely give us all things? 33 Who could bring a charge against God's chosen ones? It is God who justifies. 34 Who is he who condemns? It is Christ who died, yes rather, who was raised from the dead, who is at the right hand of God, who also makes intercession for us.

Gospel: Mark 9: 2-10

2 After six days Jesus took with him Peter, James, and John, and brought them up onto a high mountain privately by themselves, and he was changed into another form in front of them. 3 His clothing became glistening, exceedingly white, like snow, such as no launderer on earth can whiten them. 4 Elijah and Moses appeared to them, and they were talking with Jesus.
5 Peter answered Jesus, "Rabbi, it is good for us to be here. Let's make three tents: one for you, one for Moses, and one for Elijah." 6 For he didn't know what to say, for they were very afraid.
7 A cloud came, overshadowing them, and a voice came out of the cloud, "This is my beloved Son. Listen to him."
8 Suddenly looking around, they saw no one with them any more, except Jesus only.
9 As they were coming down from the mountain, he commanded them that they should tell no one what things they had seen, until after the Son of Man had risen from the

dead. 10 They kept this saying to themselves, questioning what the "rising from the dead" meant.

1. Invite the Holy Spirit into this reading, asking the Author of Scripture to speak to you through His Word
2. Read today's passage as many times as you need, take your time
3. Write down (below) what the Lord is saying to you today
4. Live with this Word in your heart through the day

_____

_____

Sunday, March 3, 2024
Third Sunday of Lent

First Reading: Exodus 20: 1-17

1 God† spoke all these words, saying, 2 "I am Yahweh your God, who brought you out of the land of Egypt, out of the house of bondage.
3 "You shall have no other gods before me.
4 "You shall not make for yourselves an idol, nor any image of anything that is in the heavens above, or that is in the earth beneath, or that is in the water under the earth:
5 you shall not bow yourself down to them, nor serve them, for I, Yahweh your God, am a jealous God, visiting the iniquity of the fathers on the children, on the third and on the fourth generation of those who hate me, 6 and showing loving kindness to thousands of those who love me and keep my commandments.
7 "You shall not misuse the name of Yahweh your God,‡ for Yahweh will not hold him guiltless who misuses his name.
8 "Remember the Sabbath day, to keep it holy. 9 You shall labor six days, and do all your work, 10 but the seventh day is a Sabbath to Yahweh your God. You shall not do any work in it, you, nor your son, nor your daughter, your male servant, nor your female servant, nor your livestock, nor your stranger who is within your gates; 11 for in six days Yahweh made heaven and earth, the sea, and all that is in them, and rested the seventh day; therefore Yahweh blessed the Sabbath day, and made it holy.

12 "Honor your father and your mother, that your days may be long in the land which Yahweh your God gives you.
13 "You shall not murder.
14 "You shall not commit adultery.
15 "You shall not steal.
16 "You shall not give false testimony against your neighbor.
17 "You shall not covet your neighbor's house. You shall not covet your neighbor's wife, nor his male servant, nor his female servant, nor his ox, nor his donkey, nor anything that is your neighbor's."

Responsorial Psalm: Psalms 19: 8-11

8 Yahweh's precepts are right, rejoicing the heart.
Yahweh's commandment is pure, enlightening the eyes.
9 The fear of Yahweh is clean, enduring forever.
Yahweh's ordinances are true, and righteous altogether.
10 They are more to be desired than gold, yes, than much fine gold,
sweeter also than honey and the extract of the honeycomb.
11 Moreover your servant is warned by them.
In keeping them there is great reward.

Second Reading: First Corinthians 1: 22-25

22 For Jews ask for signs, Greeks seek after wisdom, 23 but we preach Christ crucified, a stumbling block to Jews and foolishness to Greeks, 24 but to those who are called, both Jews and Greeks, Christ is the power of God and the wisdom of God; 25 because the foolishness of God is wiser than men, and the weakness of God is stronger than men.

Gospel: John 2: 13-25

13 The Passover of the Jews was at hand, and Jesus went up to Jerusalem. 14 He found in the temple those who sold oxen, sheep, and doves, and the changers of money sitting. 15 He made a whip of cords and drove all out of the temple, both the sheep and the oxen; and he poured out the changers' money and overthrew their tables. 16 To

those who sold the doves, he said, "Take these things out of here! Don't make my Father's house a marketplace!" 17 His disciples remembered that it was written, "Zeal for your house will eat me up."*

18 The Jews therefore answered him, "What sign do you show us, seeing that you do these things?"

19 Jesus answered them, "Destroy this temple, and in three days I will raise it up."

20 The Jews therefore said, "It took forty-six years to build this temple! Will you raise it up in three days?" 21 But he spoke of the temple of his body. 22 When therefore he was raised from the dead, his disciples remembered that he said this, and they believed the Scripture and the word which Jesus had said.

23 Now when he was in Jerusalem at the Passover, during the feast, many believed in his name, observing his signs which he did. 24 But Jesus didn't entrust himself to them, because he knew everyone, 25 and because he didn't need for anyone to testify concerning man; for he himself knew what was in man.

1. Invite the Holy Spirit into this reading, asking the Author of Scripture to speak to you through His Word
2. Read today's passage as many times as you need, take your time
3. Write down (below) what the Lord is saying to you today
4. Live with this Word in your heart through the day

_____

_____

Sunday, March 10, 2024
Fourth Sunday Of Lent

First Reading: Second Chronicles 36: 14-16, 19-23

14 Moreover all the chiefs of the priests and the people trespassed very greatly after all the abominations of the nations; and they polluted Yahweh's house which he had made holy in Jerusalem.

15 Yahweh, the God of their fathers, sent to them by his messengers, rising up early and sending, because he had compassion on his people and on his dwelling place; 16

but they mocked the messengers of God, despised his words, and scoffed at his prophets, until Yahweh's wrath arose against his people, until there was no remedy.
19 They burned God's house, broke down the wall of Jerusalem, burned all its palaces with fire, and destroyed all of its valuable vessels. 20 He carried those who had escaped from the sword away to Babylon, and they were servants to him and his sons until the reign of the kingdom of Persia, 21 to fulfill Yahweh's word by Jeremiah's mouth, until the land had enjoyed its Sabbaths. As long as it lay desolate, it kept Sabbath, to fulfill seventy years.
22 Now in the first year of Cyrus king of Persia, that Yahweh's word by the mouth of Jeremiah might be accomplished, Yahweh stirred up the spirit of Cyrus king of Persia, so that he made a proclamation throughout all his kingdom, and put it also in writing, saying, 23 "Cyrus king of Persia says, 'Yahweh, the God of heaven, has given all the kingdoms of the earth to me; and he has commanded me to build him a house in Jerusalem, which is in Judah. Whoever there is among you of all his people, Yahweh his God be with him, and let him go up.' "

Responsorial Psalm: Psalms 137: 1-6

1 By the rivers of Babylon, there we sat down.
Yes, we wept, when we remembered Zion.
2 On the willows in that land,
we hung up our harps.
3 For there, those who led us captive asked us for songs.
Those who tormented us demanded songs of joy:
"Sing us one of the songs of Zion!"
4 How can we sing Yahweh's song in a foreign land?
5 If I forget you, Jerusalem,
let my right hand forget its skill.
6 Let my tongue stick to the roof of my mouth if I don't remember you,
if I don't prefer Jerusalem above my chief joy.

Second Reading: Ephesians 2: 4-10

4 But God, being rich in mercy, for his great love with which he loved us, 5 even when we were dead through our trespasses, made us alive together with Christ—by grace you have been saved— 6 and raised us up with him, and made us to sit with him in the

heavenly places in Christ Jesus, 7 that in the ages to come he might show the exceeding riches of his grace in kindness toward us in Christ Jesus; 8 for by grace you have been saved through faith, and that not of yourselves; it is the gift of God, 9 not of works, that no one would boast. 10 For we are his workmanship, created in Christ Jesus for good works, which God prepared before that we would walk in them.

Gospel: John 3: 14-21

14 As Moses lifted up the serpent in the wilderness, even so must the Son of Man be lifted up, 15 that whoever believes in him should not perish, but have eternal life. 16 For God so loved the world, that he gave his only born§ Son, that whoever believes in him should not perish, but have eternal life. 17 For God didn't send his Son into the world to judge the world, but that the world should be saved through him. 18 He who believes in him is not judged. He who doesn't believe has been judged already, because he has not believed in the name of the only born Son of God. 19 This is the judgment, that the light has come into the world, and men loved the darkness rather than the light, for their works were evil. 20 For everyone who does evil hates the light and doesn't come to the light, lest his works would be exposed. 21 But he who does the truth comes to the light, that his works may be revealed, that they have been done in God."

1. Invite the Holy Spirit into this reading, asking the Author of Scripture to speak to you through His Word
2. Read today's passage as many times as you need, take your time
3. Write down (below) what the Lord is saying to you today
4. Live with this Word in your heart through the day

_____

_____

Sunday, March 17, 2024
Fifth Sunday of Lent

First Reading: Jeremiah 31: 31-34

31 "Behold, the days come," says Yahweh, "that I will make a new covenant with the house of Israel, and with the house of Judah, 32 not according to the covenant that I made with their fathers in the day that I took them by the hand to bring them out of the land of Egypt, which covenant of mine they broke, although I was a husband to them," says Yahweh. 33 "But this is the covenant that I will make with the house of Israel after those days," says Yahweh:
"I will put my law in their inward parts,
and I will write it in their heart.
I will be their God,
and they shall be my people.
34 They will no longer each teach his neighbor,
and every man teach his brother, saying, 'Know Yahweh;'
for they will all know me,
from their least to their greatest," says Yahweh,
"for I will forgive their iniquity,
and I will remember their sin no more."

Responsorial Psalm: Psalms 51: 3-4, 12-15

3 For I know my transgressions.
My sin is constantly before me.
4 Against you, and you only, I have sinned,
and done that which is evil in your sight,
so you may be proved right when you speak,
and justified when you judge.
12 Restore to me the joy of your salvation.
Uphold me with a willing spirit.
13 Then I will teach transgressors your ways.
Sinners will be converted to you.
14 Deliver me from the guilt of bloodshed, O God, the God of my salvation.
My tongue will sing aloud of your righteousness.
15 Lord, open my lips.
My mouth will declare your praise.

Second Reading: Hebrews 5: 7-9

7 He, in the days of his flesh, having offered up prayers and petitions with strong crying and tears to him who was able to save him from death, and having been heard for his godly fear, 8 though he was a Son, yet learned obedience by the things which he suffered. 9 Having been made perfect, he became to all of those who obey him the author of eternal salvation

Gospel: John 12: 20-33

20 Now there were certain Greeks among those who went up to worship at the feast. 21 Therefore, these came to Philip, who was from Bethsaida of Galilee, and asked him, saying, "Sir, we want to see Jesus." 22 Philip came and told Andrew, and in turn, Andrew came with Philip, and they told Jesus.

23 Jesus answered them, "The time has come for the Son of Man to be glorified. 24 Most certainly I tell you, unless a grain of wheat falls into the earth and dies, it remains by itself alone. But if it dies, it bears much fruit. 25 He who loves his life will lose it. He who hates his life in this world will keep it to eternal life. 26 If anyone serves me, let him follow me. Where I am, there my servant will also be. If anyone serves me, the Father will honor him.

27 "Now my soul is troubled. What shall I say? 'Father, save me from this time'? But I came to this time for this cause. 28 Father, glorify your name!"

Then a voice came out of the sky, saying, "I have both glorified it and will glorify it again."

29 Therefore the multitude who stood by and heard it said that it had thundered. Others said, "An angel has spoken to him."

30 Jesus answered, "This voice hasn't come for my sake, but for your sakes. 31 Now is the judgment of this world. Now the prince of this world will be cast out. 32 And I, if I am lifted up from the earth, will draw all people to myself." 33 But he said this, signifying by what kind of death he should die.

1. Invite the Holy Spirit into this reading, asking the Author of Scripture to speak to you through His Word
2. Read today's passage as many times as you need, take your time
3. Write down (below) what the Lord is saying to you today
4. Live with this Word in your heart through the day

Tuesday, March 19, 2024
Saint Joseph, Spouse of The Blessed Virgin Mary

First Reading: Second Samuel 7: 4-5a, 12-14a, 16

4 That same night, Yahweh's word came to Nathan, saying, 5 "Go and tell my servant David, 'Yahweh says, 12 When your days are fulfilled and you sleep with your fathers, I will set up your offspring after you, who will proceed out of your body, and I will establish his kingdom. 13 He will build a house for my name, and I will establish the throne of his kingdom forever. 14 I will be his father, and he will be my son.
16 Your house and your kingdom will be made sure forever before you. Your throne will be established forever."

Responsorial Psalm: Psalms 89: 2-5, 27 and 29

2 I indeed declare, "Love stands firm forever.
You established the heavens.
Your faithfulness is in them."

3 "I have made a covenant with my chosen one,
I have sworn to David, my servant,
4 'I will establish your offspring forever,
and build up your throne to all generations.' "
5 The heavens will praise your wonders, Yahweh,
your faithfulness also in the assembly of the holy ones.

27 I will also appoint him my firstborn,
the highest of the kings of the earth.
29 I will also make his offspring endure forever,
and his throne as the days of heaven.

Second Reading: Romans 4: 13, 16-18, 22

13 For the promise to Abraham and to his offspring that he would be heir of the world wasn't through the law, but through the righteousness of faith.

16 For this cause it is of faith, that it may be according to grace, to the end that the promise may be sure to all the offspring, not to that only which is of the law, but to that also which is of the faith of Abraham, who is the father of us all. 17 As it is written, "I have made you a father of many nations."* This is in the presence of him whom he believed: God, who gives life to the dead, and calls the things that are not, as though they were. 18 Against hope, Abraham in hope believed, to the end that he might become a father of many nations, according to that which had been spoken, "So will your offspring be."
22 Therefore it also was "credited to him for righteousness."

Gospel: Matthew 1: 16, 18-21, 24

16 Jacob became the father of Joseph, the husband of Mary, from whom was born Jesus,§ who is called Christ.
18 Now the birth of Jesus Christ was like this: After his mother, Mary, was engaged to Joseph, before they came together, she was found pregnant by the Holy Spirit. 19 Joseph, her husband, being a righteous man, and not willing to make her a public example, intended to put her away secretly. 20 But when he thought about these things, behold,† an angel of the Lord appeared to him in a dream, saying, "Joseph, son of David, don't be afraid to take to yourself Mary as your wife, for that which is conceived in her is of the Holy Spirit. 21 She shall give birth to a son. You shall name him Jesus,‡ for it is he who shall save his people from their sins."
24 Joseph arose from his sleep, and did as the angel of the Lord commanded him, and took his wife to himself; 25 and didn't know her sexually until she had given birth to her firstborn son. He named him Jesus.

1. Invite the Holy Spirit into this reading, asking the Author of Scripture to speak to you through His Word
2. Read today's passage as many times as you need, take your time
3. Write down (below) what the Lord is saying to you today
4. Live with this Word in your heart through the day

_____
_____

Sunday, March 24, 2024
PALM SUNDAY OF THE PASSION OF THE LORD

Procession: Mark 11: 1-10

1 When they came near to Jerusalem, to Bethsphage† and Bethany, at the Mount of Olives, he sent two of his disciples 2 and said to them, "Go your way into the village that is opposite you. Immediately as you enter into it, you will find a young donkey tied, on which no one has sat. Untie him and bring him. 3 If anyone asks you, 'Why are you doing this?' say, 'The Lord needs him;' and immediately he will send him back here."
4 They went away, and found a young donkey tied at the door outside in the open street, and they untied him. 5 Some of those who stood there asked them, "What are you doing, untying the young donkey?" 6 They said to them just as Jesus had said, and they let them go.
7 They brought the young donkey to Jesus and threw their garments on it, and Jesus sat on it. 8 Many spread their garments on the way, and others were cutting down branches from the trees and spreading them on the road. 9 Those who went in front and those who followed cried out, "Hosanna!‡ Blessed is he who comes in the name of the Lord!* 10 Blessed is the kingdom of our father David that is coming in the name of the Lord! Hosanna in the highest!"

First Reading: Isaiah 50: 4-7

4 The Lord Yahweh has given me the tongue of those who are taught,
that I may know how to sustain with words him who is weary.
He awakens morning by morning,
he awakens my ear to hear as those who are taught.
5 The Lord Yahweh has opened my ear.
I was not rebellious.
I have not turned back.
6 I gave my back to those who beat me,
and my cheeks to those who plucked off the hair.
I didn't hide my face from shame and spitting.
7 For the Lord Yahweh will help me.
Therefore I have not been confounded.

Therefore I have set my face like a flint,
and I know that I won't be disappointed.

Responsorial Psalm: Psalms 22: 8-9, 17-20, 23-24

8 "He trusts in Yahweh.
Let him deliver him.
Let him rescue him, since he delights in him."
9 But you brought me out of the womb.
You made me trust while at my mother's breasts.
17 I can count all of my bones.
They look and stare at me.
18 They divide my garments among them.
They cast lots for my clothing.
19 But don't be far off, Yahweh.
You are my help. Hurry to help me!
20 Deliver my soul from the sword,
my precious life from the power of the dog.
23 You who fear Yahweh, praise him!
All you descendants of Jacob, glorify him!
Stand in awe of him, all you descendants of Israel!
24 For he has not despised nor abhorred the affliction of the afflicted,
neither has he hidden his face from him;
but when he cried to him, he heard.

Second Reading: Philippians 2: 6-11

6 who, existing in the form of God, didn't consider equality with God a thing to be grasped, 7 but emptied himself, taking the form of a servant, being made in the likeness of men. 8 And being found in human form, he humbled himself, becoming obedient to the point of death, yes, the death of the cross. 9 Therefore God also highly exalted him, and gave to him the name which is above every name, 10 that at the name of Jesus every knee should bow, of those in heaven, those on earth, and those under the earth, 11 and that every tongue should confess that Jesus Christ is Lord, to the glory of God the Father.

Gospel: Mark 14: 1 – 15: 47

1 It was now two days before the Passover and the Feast of Unleavened Bread, and the chief priests and the scribes sought how they might seize him by deception and kill him. 2 For they said, "Not during the feast, because there might be a riot among the people."
3 While he was at Bethany, in the house of Simon the leper, as he sat at the table, a woman came having an alabaster jar of ointment of pure nard—very costly. She broke the jar and poured it over his head. 4 But there were some who were indignant among themselves, saying, "Why has this ointment been wasted? 5 For this might have been sold for more than three hundred denarii† and given to the poor." So they grumbled against her.
6 But Jesus said, "Leave her alone. Why do you trouble her? She has done a good work for me. 7 For you always have the poor with you, and whenever you want to, you can do them good; but you will not always have me. 8 She has done what she could. She has anointed my body beforehand for the burying. 9 Most certainly I tell you, wherever this Good News may be preached throughout the whole world, that which this woman has done will also be spoken of for a memorial of her."
10 Judas Iscariot, who was one of the twelve, went away to the chief priests, that he might deliver him to them. 11 They, when they heard it, were glad, and promised to give him money. He sought how he might conveniently deliver him.
12 On the first day of unleavened bread, when they sacrificed the Passover, his disciples asked him, "Where do you want us to go and prepare that you may eat the Passover?"
13 He sent two of his disciples and said to them, "Go into the city, and there a man carrying a pitcher of water will meet you. Follow him, 14 and wherever he enters in, tell the master of the house, 'The Teacher says, "Where is the guest room, where I may eat the Passover with my disciples?" ' 15 He will himself show you a large upper room furnished and ready. Get ready for us there."
16 His disciples went out, and came into the city, and found things as he had said to them, and they prepared the Passover.
17 When it was evening he came with the twelve. 18 As they sat and were eating, Jesus said, "Most certainly I tell you, one of you will betray me—he who eats with me."
19 They began to be sorrowful, and to ask him one by one, "Surely not I?" And another said, "Surely not I?"
20 He answered them, "It is one of the twelve, he who dips with me in the dish. 21 For the Son of Man goes as it is written about him, but woe to that man by whom the Son of Man is betrayed! It would be better for that man if he had not been born."

22 As they were eating, Jesus took bread, and when he had blessed it, he broke it and gave to them, and said, "Take, eat. This is my body."

23 He took the cup, and when he had given thanks, he gave to them. They all drank of it. 24 He said to them, "This is my blood of the new covenant, which is poured out for many. 25 Most certainly I tell you, I will no more drink of the fruit of the vine until that day when I drink it anew in God's Kingdom." 26 When they had sung a hymn, they went out to the Mount of Olives.

27 Jesus said to them, "All of you will be made to stumble because of me tonight, for it is written, 'I will strike the shepherd, and the sheep will be scattered.'* 28 However, after I am raised up, I will go before you into Galilee."

29 But Peter said to him, "Although all will be offended, yet I will not."

30 Jesus said to him, "Most certainly I tell you that you today, even this night, before the rooster crows twice, you will deny me three times."

31 But he spoke all the more, "If I must die with you, I will not deny you." They all said the same thing.

32 They came to a place which was named Gethsemane. He said to his disciples, "Sit here while I pray." 33 He took with him Peter, James, and John, and began to be greatly troubled and distressed. 34 He said to them, "My soul is exceedingly sorrowful, even to death. Stay here and watch."

35 He went forward a little, and fell on the ground, and prayed that if it were possible, the hour might pass away from him. 36 He said, "Abba,‡ Father, all things are possible to you. Please remove this cup from me. However, not what I desire, but what you desire."

37 He came and found them sleeping, and said to Peter, "Simon, are you sleeping? Couldn't you watch one hour? 38 Watch and pray, that you may not enter into temptation. The spirit indeed is willing, but the flesh is weak."

39 Again he went away and prayed, saying the same words. 40 Again he returned and found them sleeping, for their eyes were very heavy; and they didn't know what to answer him. 41 He came the third time and said to them, "Sleep on now, and take your rest. It is enough. The hour has come. Behold, the Son of Man is betrayed into the hands of sinners. 42 Arise! Let's get going. Behold, he who betrays me is at hand."

43 Immediately, while he was still speaking, Judas, one of the twelve, came—and with him a multitude with swords and clubs, from the chief priests, the scribes, and the elders. 44 Now he who betrayed him had given them a sign, saying, "Whomever I will kiss, that is he. Seize him, and lead him away safely." 45 When he had come, immediately he came to him and said, "Rabbi! Rabbi!" and kissed him. 46 They laid their hands on him and seized him. 47 But a certain one of those who stood by drew his sword and struck the servant of the high priest, and cut off his ear.

48 Jesus answered them, "Have you come out, as against a robber, with swords and clubs to seize me? 49 I was daily with you in the temple teaching, and you didn't arrest me. But this is so that the Scriptures might be fulfilled."

50 They all left him, and fled. 51 A certain young man followed him, having a linen cloth thrown around himself over his naked body. The young men grabbed him, 52 but he left the linen cloth and fled from them naked. 53 They led Jesus away to the high priest. All the chief priests, the elders, and the scribes came together with him.

54 Peter had followed him from a distance, until he came into the court of the high priest. He was sitting with the officers, and warming himself in the light of the fire. 55 Now the chief priests and the whole council sought witnesses against Jesus to put him to death, and found none. 56 For many gave false testimony against him, and their testimony didn't agree with each other. 57 Some stood up and gave false testimony against him, saying, 58 "We heard him say, 'I will destroy this temple that is made with hands, and in three days I will build another made without hands.' " 59 Even so, their testimony didn't agree.

60 The high priest stood up in the middle, and asked Jesus, "Have you no answer? What is it which these testify against you?" 61 But he stayed quiet, and answered nothing. Again the high priest asked him, "Are you the Christ, the Son of the Blessed?" 62 Jesus said, "I am. You will see the Son of Man sitting at the right hand of Power, and coming with the clouds of the sky."

63 The high priest tore his clothes and said, "What further need have we of witnesses? 64 You have heard the blasphemy! What do you think?" They all condemned him to be worthy of death. 65 Some began to spit on him, and to cover his face, and to beat him with fists, and to tell him, "Prophesy!" The officers struck him with the palms of their hands.

66 As Peter was in the courtyard below, one of the maids of the high priest came, 67 and seeing Peter warming himself, she looked at him and said, "You were also with the Nazarene, Jesus!"

68 But he denied it, saying, "I neither know nor understand what you are saying." He went out on the porch, and the rooster crowed.

69 The maid saw him and began again to tell those who stood by, "This is one of them." 70 But he again denied it. After a little while again those who stood by said to Peter, "You truly are one of them, for you are a Galilean, and your speech shows it." 71 But he began to curse and to swear, "I don't know this man of whom you speak!"

72 The rooster crowed the second time. Peter remembered the words that Jesus said to him, "Before the rooster crows twice, you will deny me three times." When he thought about that, he wept.

1 Immediately in the morning the chief priests, with the elders, scribes, and the whole council, held a consultation, bound Jesus, carried him away, and delivered him up to Pilate. 2 Pilate asked him, "Are you the King of the Jews?"

He answered, "So you say."

3 The chief priests accused him of many things. 4 Pilate again asked him, "Have you no answer? See how many things they testify against you!"

5 But Jesus made no further answer, so that Pilate marveled.

6 Now at the feast he used to release to them one prisoner, whomever they asked of him. 7 There was one called Barabbas, bound with his fellow insurgents, men who in the insurrection had committed murder. 8 The multitude, crying aloud, began to ask him to do as he always did for them. 9 Pilate answered them, saying, "Do you want me to release to you the King of the Jews?" 10 For he perceived that for envy the chief priests had delivered him up. 11 But the chief priests stirred up the multitude, that he should release Barabbas to them instead. 12 Pilate again asked them, "What then should I do to him whom you call the King of the Jews?"

13 They cried out again, "Crucify him!"

14 Pilate said to them, "Why, what evil has he done?"

But they cried out exceedingly, "Crucify him!"

15 Pilate, wishing to please the multitude, released Barabbas to them, and handed over Jesus, when he had flogged him, to be crucified.

16 The soldiers led him away within the court, which is the Praetorium; and they called together the whole cohort. 17 They clothed him with purple; and weaving a crown of thorns, they put it on him. 18 They began to salute him, "Hail, King of the Jews!" 19 They struck his head with a reed and spat on him, and bowing their knees, did homage to him. 20 When they had mocked him, they took the purple cloak off him, and put his own garments on him. They led him out to crucify him.

21 They compelled one passing by, coming from the country, Simon of Cyrene, the father of Alexander and Rufus, to go with them that he might bear his cross. 22 They brought him to the place called Golgotha, which is, being interpreted, "The place of a skull." 23 They offered him wine mixed with myrrh to drink, but he didn't take it.

24 Crucifying him, they parted his garments among them, casting lots on them, what each should take. 25 It was the third hour† when they crucified him. 26 The superscription of his accusation was written over him: "THE KING OF THE JEWS." 27 With him they crucified two robbers, one on his right hand, and one on his left. 28 The Scripture was fulfilled which says, "He was counted with transgressors."‡

29 Those who passed by blasphemed him, wagging their heads and saying, "Ha! You who destroy the temple and build it in three days, 30 save yourself, and come down from the cross!"

31 Likewise, also the chief priests mocking among themselves with the scribes said, "He saved others. He can't save himself. 32 Let the Christ, the King of Israel, now come down from the cross, that we may see and believe him."§ Those who were crucified with him also insulted him.

33 When the sixth hour† had come, there was darkness over the whole land until the ninth hour.‡ 34 At the ninth hour Jesus cried with a loud voice, saying, "Eloi, Eloi, lama sabachthani?" which is, being interpreted, "My God, my God, why have you forsaken me?" *

35 Some of those who stood by, when they heard it, said, "Behold, he is calling Elijah." 36 One ran, and filling a sponge full of vinegar, put it on a reed and gave it to him to drink, saying, "Let him be. Let's see whether Elijah comes to take him down."

37 Jesus cried out with a loud voice, and gave up the spirit. 38 The veil of the temple was torn in two from the top to the bottom. 39 When the centurion, who stood by opposite him, saw that he cried out like this and breathed his last, he said, "Truly this man was the Son of God!"

40 There were also women watching from afar, among whom were both Mary Magdalene and Mary the mother of James the less and of Joses, and Salome; 41 who, when he was in Galilee, followed him and served him; and many other women who came up with him to Jerusalem.

42 When evening had now come, because it was the Preparation Day, that is, the day before the Sabbath, 43 Joseph of Arimathaea, a prominent council member who also himself was looking for God's Kingdom, came. He boldly went in to Pilate, and asked for Jesus' body. 44 Pilate was surprised to hear that he was already dead; and summoning the centurion, he asked him whether he had been dead long. 45 When he found out from the centurion, he granted the body to Joseph. 46 He bought a linen cloth, and taking him down, wound him in the linen cloth and laid him in a tomb which had been cut out of a rock. He rolled a stone against the door of the tomb. 47 Mary Magdalene and Mary the mother of Joses, saw where he was laid.

1. Invite the Holy Spirit into this reading, asking the Author of Scripture to speak to you through His Word
2. Read today's passage as many times as you need, take your time
3. Write down (below) what the Lord is saying to you today
4. Live with this Word in your heart through the day

_____

_____

Thursday, March 28, 2024
Thursday of Holy Week (Holy Thursday)

First Reading: Exodus 12: 1-8, 11-14

1 Yahweh spoke to Moses and Aaron in the land of Egypt, saying, 2 "This month shall be to you the beginning of months. It shall be the first month of the year to you. 3 Speak to all the congregation of Israel, saying, 'On the tenth day of this month, they shall take to them every man a lamb, according to their fathers' houses, a lamb for a household; 4 and if the household is too little for a lamb, then he and his neighbor next to his house shall take one according to the number of the souls. You shall make your count for the lamb according to what everyone can eat. 5 Your lamb shall be without defect, a male a year old. You shall take it from the sheep or from the goats. 6 You shall keep it until the fourteenth day of the same month; and the whole assembly of the congregation of Israel shall kill it at evening. 7 They shall take some of the blood, and put it on the two door posts and on the lintel, on the houses in which they shall eat it. 8 They shall eat the meat in that night, roasted with fire, with unleavened bread. They shall eat it with bitter herbs.
11 This is how you shall eat it: with your belt on your waist, your sandals on your feet, and your staff in your hand; and you shall eat it in haste: it is Yahweh's Passover. 12 For I will go through the land of Egypt in that night, and will strike all the firstborn in the land of Egypt, both man and animal. I will execute judgments against all the gods of Egypt. I am Yahweh. 13 The blood shall be to you for a token on the houses where you are. When I see the blood, I will pass over you, and no plague will be on you to destroy you when I strike the land of Egypt. 14 This day shall be a memorial for you. You shall keep it as a feast to Yahweh. You shall keep it as a feast throughout your generations by an ordinance forever.

Responsorial Psalm: Psalms 116: 12-13, 15-18

12 What will I give to Yahweh for all his benefits toward me?
13 I will take the cup of salvation, and call on Yahweh's name.
15 Precious in Yahweh's sight is the death of his saints.
16 Yahweh, truly I am your servant.
I am your servant, the son of your servant girl.
You have freed me from my chains.

17 I will offer to you the sacrifice of thanksgiving,
and will call on Yahweh's name.
18 I will pay my vows to Yahweh,
yes, in the presence of all his people,

Second Reading: First Corinthians 11: 23-26

23 For I received from the Lord that which also I delivered to you, that the Lord Jesus on the night in which he was betrayed took bread. 24 When he had given thanks, he broke it and said, "Take, eat. This is my body, which is broken for you. Do this in memory of me." 25 In the same way he also took the cup after supper, saying, "This cup is the new covenant in my blood. Do this, as often as you drink, in memory of me." 26 For as often as you eat this bread and drink this cup, you proclaim the Lord's death until he comes.

Gospel: John 13: 1-15

1 Now before the feast of the Passover, Jesus, knowing that his time had come that he would depart from this world to the Father, having loved his own who were in the world, he loved them to the end. 2 During supper, the devil having already put into the heart of Judas Iscariot, Simon's son, to betray him, 3 Jesus, knowing that the Father had given all things into his hands, and that he came from God and was going to God, 4 arose from supper, and laid aside his outer garments. He took a towel and wrapped a towel around his waist. 5 Then he poured water into the basin, and began to wash the disciples' feet and to wipe them with the towel that was wrapped around him. 6 Then he came to Simon Peter. He said to him, "Lord, do you wash my feet?"
7 Jesus answered him, "You don't know what I am doing now, but you will understand later."
8 Peter said to him, "You will never wash my feet!"
Jesus answered him, "If I don't wash you, you have no part with me."
9 Simon Peter said to him, "Lord, not my feet only, but also my hands and my head!"
10 Jesus said to him, "Someone who has bathed only needs to have his feet washed, but is completely clean. You are clean, but not all of you." 11 For he knew him who would betray him; therefore he said, "You are not all clean." 12 So when he had washed their feet, put his outer garment back on, and sat down again, he said to them, "Do you know what I have done to you? 13 You call me, 'Teacher' and 'Lord.' You say so

correctly, for so I am. 14 If I then, the Lord and the Teacher, have washed your feet, you also ought to wash one another's feet. 15 For I have given you an example, that you should also do as I have done to you.

1. Invite the Holy Spirit into this reading, asking the Author of Scripture to speak to you through His Word
2. Read today's passage as many times as you need, take your time
3. Write down (below) what the Lord is saying to you today
4. Live with this Word in your heart through the day

_____

_____

Friday, March 29, 2024
Friday of the Passion of the Lord (Good Friday)

First Reading: Isaiah 52: 13 – 53: 12

13 Behold, my servant will deal wisely.
He will be exalted and lifted up,
and will be very high.
14 Just as many were astonished at you—
his appearance was marred more than any man, and his form more than the sons of men—
15 so he will cleanse† many nations.
Kings will shut their mouths at him;
for they will see that which had not been told them,
and they will understand that which they had not heard.
1 Who has believed our message?
To whom has Yahweh's arm been revealed?
2 For he grew up before him as a tender plant,
and as a root out of dry ground.
He has no good looks or majesty.
When we see him, there is no beauty that we should desire him.
3 He was despised

and rejected by men,
a man of suffering
and acquainted with disease.
He was despised as one from whom men hide their face;
and we didn't respect him.

4 Surely he has borne our sickness
and carried our suffering;
yet we considered him plagued,
struck by God, and afflicted.
5 But he was pierced for our transgressions.
He was crushed for our iniquities.
The punishment that brought our peace was on him;
and by his wounds we are healed.
6 All we like sheep have gone astray.
Everyone has turned to his own way;
and Yahweh has laid on him the iniquity of us all.

7 He was oppressed,
yet when he was afflicted he didn't open his mouth.
As a lamb that is led to the slaughter,
and as a sheep that before its shearers is silent,
so he didn't open his mouth.
8 He was taken away by oppression and judgment.
As for his generation,
who considered that he was cut off out of the land of the living
and stricken for the disobedience of my people?
9 They made his grave with the wicked,
and with a rich man in his death,
although he had done no violence,
nor was any deceit in his mouth.

10 Yet it pleased Yahweh to bruise him.
He has caused him to suffer.
When you make his soul an offering for sin,
he will see his offspring.
He will prolong his days
 and Yahweh's pleasure will prosper in his hand.

11 After the suffering of his soul,
he will see the light† and be satisfied.
My righteous servant will justify many by the knowledge of himself;
and he will bear their iniquities.
12 Therefore I will give him a portion with the great.
He will divide the plunder with the strong,
because he poured out his soul to death
and was counted with the transgressors;
yet he bore the sins of many
and made intercession for the transgressors.

Responsorial Psalm: Psalms 31: 2, 6, 12-13, 15-16, 17, 24

2 Bow down your ear to me.
Deliver me speedily.
Be to me a strong rock,
a house of defense to save me.
6 I hate those who regard lying vanities,
but I trust in Yahweh.
12 I am forgotten from their hearts like a dead man.
I am like broken pottery.
13 For I have heard the slander of many, terror on every side,
while they conspire together against me,
they plot to take away my life.
15 My times are in your hand.
Deliver me from the hand of my enemies, and from those who persecute me.
16 Make your face to shine on your servant.
Save me in your loving kindness.
17 Let me not be disappointed, Yahweh, for I have called on you.
Let the wicked be disappointed.
Let them be silent in Sheol
24 Be strong, and let your heart take courage,
all you who hope in Yahweh.

Second Reading: Hebrews 4: 14-16; 5: 7-9

14 Having then a great high priest who has passed through the heavens, Jesus, the Son of God, let's hold tightly to our confession. 15 For we don't have a high priest who can't be touched with the feeling of our infirmities, but one who has been in all points tempted like we are, yet without sin. 16 Let's therefore draw near with boldness to the throne of grace, that we may receive mercy and may find grace for help in time of need. 7 He, in the days of his flesh, having offered up prayers and petitions with strong crying and tears to him who was able to save him from death, and having been heard for his godly fear, 8 though he was a Son, yet learned obedience by the things which he suffered. 9 Having been made perfect, he became to all of those who obey him the author of eternal salvation

Gospel: John 18: 1 – 19: 42

1 When Jesus had spoken these words, he went out with his disciples over the brook Kidron, where there was a garden, into which he and his disciples entered. 2 Now Judas, who betrayed him, also knew the place, for Jesus often met there with his disciples. 3 Judas then, having taken a detachment of soldiers and officers from the chief priests and the Pharisees, came there with lanterns, torches, and weapons. 4 Jesus therefore, knowing all the things that were happening to him, went out and said to them, "Who are you looking for?"
5 They answered him, "Jesus of Nazareth."
Jesus said to them, "I am he."
Judas also, who betrayed him, was standing with them. 6 When therefore he said to them, "I am he," they went backward and fell to the ground.
7 Again therefore he asked them, "Who are you looking for?"
They said, "Jesus of Nazareth."
8 Jesus answered, "I told you that I am he. If therefore you seek me, let these go their way," 9 that the word might be fulfilled which he spoke, "Of those whom you have given me, I have lost none."*
10 Simon Peter therefore, having a sword, drew it, struck the high priest's servant, and cut off his right ear. The servant's name was Malchus. 11 Jesus therefore said to Peter, "Put the sword into its sheath. The cup which the Father has given me, shall I not surely drink it?"
12 So the detachment, the commanding officer, and the officers of the Jews seized Jesus and bound him, 13 and led him to Annas first, for he was father-in-law to Caiaphas, who was high priest that year. 14 Now it was Caiaphas who advised the Jews that it was expedient that one man should perish for the people.

15 Simon Peter followed Jesus, as did another disciple. Now that disciple was known to the high priest, and entered in with Jesus into the court of the high priest; 16 but Peter was standing at the door outside. So the other disciple, who was known to the high priest, went out and spoke to her who kept the door, and brought in Peter. 17 Then the maid who kept the door said to Peter, "Are you also one of this man's disciples?" He said, "I am not."

18 Now the servants and the officers were standing there, having made a fire of coals, for it was cold. They were warming themselves. Peter was with them, standing and warming himself.

19 The high priest therefore asked Jesus about his disciples and about his teaching.

20 Jesus answered him, "I spoke openly to the world. I always taught in synagogues and in the temple, where the Jews always meet. I said nothing in secret. 21 Why do you ask me? Ask those who have heard me what I said to them. Behold, they know the things which I said."

22 When he had said this, one of the officers standing by slapped Jesus with his hand, saying, "Do you answer the high priest like that?"

23 Jesus answered him, "If I have spoken evil, testify of the evil; but if well, why do you beat me?"

24 Annas sent him bound to Caiaphas, the high priest.

25 Now Simon Peter was standing and warming himself. They said therefore to him, "You aren't also one of his disciples, are you?"

He denied it and said, "I am not."

26 One of the servants of the high priest, being a relative of him whose ear Peter had cut off, said, "Didn't I see you in the garden with him?"

27 Peter therefore denied it again, and immediately the rooster crowed.

28 They led Jesus therefore from Caiaphas into the Praetorium. It was early, and they themselves didn't enter into the Praetorium, that they might not be defiled, but might eat the Passover. 29 Pilate therefore went out to them and said, "What accusation do you bring against this man?"

30 They answered him, "If this man weren't an evildoer, we wouldn't have delivered him up to you."

31 Pilate therefore said to them, "Take him yourselves, and judge him according to your law."

Therefore the Jews said to him, "It is illegal for us to put anyone to death," 32 that the word of Jesus might be fulfilled, which he spoke, signifying by what kind of death he should die.

33 Pilate therefore entered again into the Praetorium, called Jesus, and said to him, "Are you the King of the Jews?"

34 Jesus answered him, "Do you say this by yourself, or did others tell you about me?"

35 Pilate answered, "I'm not a Jew, am I? Your own nation and the chief priests delivered you to me. What have you done?"

36 Jesus answered, "My Kingdom is not of this world. If my Kingdom were of this world, then my servants would fight, that I wouldn't be delivered to the Jews. But now my Kingdom is not from here."

37 Pilate therefore said to him, "Are you a king then?"

Jesus answered, "You say that I am a king. For this reason I have been born, and for this reason I have come into the world, that I should testify to the truth. Everyone who is of the truth listens to my voice."

38 Pilate said to him, "What is truth?"

When he had said this, he went out again to the Jews, and said to them, "I find no basis for a charge against him. 39 But you have a custom that I should release someone to you at the Passover. Therefore, do you want me to release to you the King of the Jews?"

40 Then they all shouted again, saying, "Not this man, but Barabbas!" Now Barabbas was a robber.

1 So Pilate then took Jesus and flogged him. 2 The soldiers twisted thorns into a crown and put it on his head, and dressed him in a purple garment. 3 They kept saying, "Hail, King of the Jews!" and they kept slapping him.

4 Then Pilate went out again, and said to them, "Behold, I bring him out to you, that you may know that I find no basis for a charge against him."

5 Jesus therefore came out, wearing the crown of thorns and the purple garment. Pilate said to them, "Behold, the man!"

6 When therefore the chief priests and the officers saw him, they shouted, saying, "Crucify! Crucify!"

Pilate said to them, "Take him yourselves and crucify him, for I find no basis for a charge against him."

7 The Jews answered him, "We have a law, and by our law he ought to die, because he made himself the Son of God."

8 When therefore Pilate heard this saying, he was more afraid. 9 He entered into the Praetorium again, and said to Jesus, "Where are you from?" But Jesus gave him no answer. 10 Pilate therefore said to him, "Aren't you speaking to me? Don't you know that I have power to release you and have power to crucify you?"

11 Jesus answered, "You would have no power at all against me, unless it were given to you from above. Therefore he who delivered me to you has greater sin."

12 At this, Pilate was seeking to release him, but the Jews cried out, saying, "If you release this man, you aren't Caesar's friend! Everyone who makes himself a king speaks against Caesar!"

13 When Pilate therefore heard these words, he brought Jesus out and sat down on the judgment seat at a place called "The Pavement", but in Hebrew, "Gabbatha." 14 Now it was the Preparation Day of the Passover, at about the sixth hour.† He said to the Jews, "Behold, your King!"

15 They cried out, "Away with him! Away with him! Crucify him!"

Pilate said to them, "Shall I crucify your King?"

The chief priests answered, "We have no king but Caesar!"

16 So then he delivered him to them to be crucified. So they took Jesus and led him away. 17 He went out, bearing his cross, to the place called "The Place of a Skull", which is called in Hebrew, "Golgotha", 18 where they crucified him, and with him two others, on either side one, and Jesus in the middle. 19 Pilate wrote a title also, and put it on the cross. There was written, "JESUS OF NAZARETH, THE KING OF THE JEWS." 20 Therefore many of the Jews read this title, for the place where Jesus was crucified was near the city; and it was written in Hebrew, in Latin, and in Greek. 21 The chief priests of the Jews therefore said to Pilate, "Don't write, 'The King of the Jews,' but, 'he said, "I am King of the Jews." ' "

22 Pilate answered, "What I have written, I have written."

23 Then the soldiers, when they had crucified Jesus, took his garments and made four parts, to every soldier a part; and also the tunic. Now the tunic was without seam, woven from the top throughout. 24 Then they said to one another, "Let's not tear it, but cast lots for it to decide whose it will be," that the Scripture might be fulfilled, which says,

"They parted my garments among them.

They cast lots for my clothing."*

Therefore the soldiers did these things.

25 But standing by Jesus' cross were his mother, his mother's sister, Mary the wife of Clopas, and Mary Magdalene. 26 Therefore when Jesus saw his mother, and the disciple whom he loved standing there, he said to his mother, "Woman, behold, your son!" 27 Then he said to the disciple, "Behold, your mother!" From that hour, the disciple took her to his own home.

28 After this, Jesus, seeing‡ that all things were now finished, that the Scripture might be fulfilled, said, "I am thirsty!" 29 Now a vessel full of vinegar was set there; so they put a sponge full of the vinegar on hyssop, and held it at his mouth. 30 When Jesus therefore had received the vinegar, he said, "It is finished!" Then he bowed his head and gave up his spirit.

31 Therefore the Jews, because it was the Preparation Day, so that the bodies wouldn't remain on the cross on the Sabbath (for that Sabbath was a special one), asked of Pilate that their legs might be broken and that they might be taken away. 32 Therefore the

soldiers came and broke the legs of the first and of the other who was crucified with him; 33 but when they came to Jesus and saw that he was already dead, they didn't break his legs. 34 However, one of the soldiers pierced his side with a spear, and immediately blood and water came out. 35 He who has seen has testified, and his testimony is true. He knows that he tells the truth, that you may believe. 36 For these things happened that the Scripture might be fulfilled, "A bone of him will not be broken."* 37 Again another Scripture says, "They will look on him whom they pierced."*

38 After these things, Joseph of Arimathaea, being a disciple of Jesus, but secretly for fear of the Jews, asked of Pilate that he might take away Jesus' body. Pilate gave him permission. He came therefore and took away his body. 39 Nicodemus, who at first came to Jesus by night, also came bringing a mixture of myrrh and aloes, about a hundred Roman pounds.§ 40 So they took Jesus' body, and bound it in linen cloths with the spices, as the custom of the Jews is to bury. 41 Now in the place where he was crucified there was a garden. In the garden was a new tomb in which no man had ever yet been laid. 42 Then, because of the Jews' Preparation Day (for the tomb was near at hand), they laid Jesus there.

1. Invite the Holy Spirit into this reading, asking the Author of Scripture to speak to you through His Word
2. Read today's passage as many times as you need, take your time
3. Write down (below) what the Lord is saying to you today
4. Live with this Word in your heart through the day

_____

_____

Saturday, March 30, 2024
Holy Saturday

First Reading: Genesis 1: 1, 26-31a

1 In the beginning, God† created the heavens and the earth. 2 The earth was formless and empty. Darkness was on the surface of the deep and God's Spirit was hovering over the surface of the waters.

26 God said, "Let's make man in our image, after our likeness. Let them have dominion over the fish of the sea, and over the birds of the sky, and over the livestock, and over all the earth, and over every creeping thing that creeps on the earth." 27 God created man in his own image. In God's image he created him; male and female he created them. 28 God blessed them. God said to them, "Be fruitful, multiply, fill the earth, and subdue it. Have dominion over the fish of the sea, over the birds of the sky, and over every living thing that moves on the earth." 29 God said, "Behold,‡ I have given you every herb yielding seed, which is on the surface of all the earth, and every tree, which bears fruit yielding seed. It will be your food. 30 To every animal of the earth, and to every bird of the sky, and to everything that creeps on the earth, in which there is life, I have given every green herb for food;" and it was so.
31 God saw everything that he had made, and, behold, it was very good.

Responsorial Psalm: Psalms 104: 1-2, 5-6, 10, 12-14, 24, 35

1 Bless Yahweh, my soul.
Yahweh, my God, you are very great.
You are clothed with honor and majesty.
2 He covers himself with light as with a garment.
He stretches out the heavens like a curtain.
5 He laid the foundations of the earth,
that it should not be moved forever.
6 You covered it with the deep as with a cloak.
The waters stood above the mountains.
10 He sends springs into the valleys.
They run among the mountains.
12 The birds of the sky nest by them.
They sing among the branches.
13 He waters the mountains from his rooms.
The earth is filled with the fruit of your works.
14 He causes the grass to grow for the livestock,
and plants for man to cultivate,
that he may produce food out of the earth:
24 Yahweh, how many are your works!
In wisdom, you have made them all.
The earth is full of your riches.
35 Let sinners be consumed out of the earth.

Let the wicked be no more.
Bless Yahweh, my soul.
Praise Yah!

Second Reading: Genesis 22: 1-18

1 After these things, God tested Abraham, and said to him, "Abraham!"
He said, "Here I am."
2 He said, "Now take your son, your only son, Isaac, whom you love, and go into the land of Moriah. Offer him there as a burnt offering on one of the mountains which I will tell you of."
3 Abraham rose early in the morning, and saddled his donkey; and took two of his young men with him, and Isaac his son. He split the wood for the burnt offering, and rose up, and went to the place of which God had told him. 4 On the third day Abraham lifted up his eyes, and saw the place far off. 5 Abraham said to his young men, "Stay here with the donkey. The boy and I will go over there. We will worship, and come back to you." 6 Abraham took the wood of the burnt offering and laid it on Isaac his son. He took in his hand the fire and the knife. They both went together. 7 Isaac spoke to Abraham his father, and said, "My father?"
He said, "Here I am, my son."
He said, "Here is the fire and the wood, but where is the lamb for a burnt offering?"
8 Abraham said, "God will provide himself the lamb for a burnt offering, my son." So they both went together. 9 They came to the place which God had told him of. Abraham built the altar there, and laid the wood in order, bound Isaac his son, and laid him on the altar, on the wood. 10 Abraham stretched out his hand, and took the knife to kill his son.
11 Yahweh's angel called to him out of the sky, and said, "Abraham, Abraham!"
He said, "Here I am."
12 He said, "Don't lay your hand on the boy or do anything to him. For now I know that you fear God, since you have not withheld your son, your only son, from me."
13 Abraham lifted up his eyes, and looked, and saw that behind him was a ram caught in the thicket by his horns. Abraham went and took the ram, and offered him up for a burnt offering instead of his son. 14 Abraham called the name of that place "Yahweh Will Provide".† As it is said to this day, "On Yahweh's mountain, it will be provided."
15 Yahweh's angel called to Abraham a second time out of the sky, 16 and said, " 'I have sworn by myself,' says Yahweh, 'because you have done this thing, and have not withheld your son, your only son, 17 that I will bless you greatly, and I will multiply

your offspring greatly like the stars of the heavens, and like the sand which is on the seashore. Your offspring will possess the gate of his enemies. 18 All the nations of the earth will be blessed by your offspring, because you have obeyed my voice.' "

Responsorial Psalm: Psalms 16: 5, 8-11

5 Yahweh assigned my portion and my cup.
You made my lot secure.
8 I have set Yahweh always before me.
Because he is at my right hand, I shall not be moved.
9 Therefore my heart is glad, and my tongue rejoices.
My body shall also dwell in safety.
10 For you will not leave my soul in Sheol,†
neither will you allow your holy one to see corruption.
11 You will show me the path of life.
In your presence is fullness of joy.
In your right hand there are pleasures forever more.

Third Reading: Exodus 14: 15 – 15: 1

15 Yahweh said to Moses, "Why do you cry to me? Speak to the children of Israel, that they go forward. 16 Lift up your rod, and stretch out your hand over the sea and divide it. Then the children of Israel shall go into the middle of the sea on dry ground. 17 Behold, I myself will harden the hearts of the Egyptians, and they will go in after them. I will get myself honor over Pharaoh, and over all his armies, over his chariots, and over his horsemen. 18 The Egyptians shall know that I am Yahweh when I have gotten myself honor over Pharaoh, over his chariots, and over his horsemen." 19 The angel of God, who went before the camp of Israel, moved and went behind them; and the pillar of cloud moved from before them, and stood behind them. 20 It came between the camp of Egypt and the camp of Israel. There was the cloud and the darkness, yet it gave light by night. One didn't come near the other all night.
21 Moses stretched out his hand over the sea, and Yahweh caused the sea to go back by a strong east wind all night, and made the sea dry land, and the waters were divided. 22 The children of Israel went into the middle of the sea on the dry ground; and the waters were a wall to them on their right hand and on their left. 23 The Egyptians pursued, and went in after them into the middle of the sea: all of Pharaoh's horses, his

chariots, and his horsemen. 24 In the morning watch, Yahweh looked out on the Egyptian army through the pillar of fire and of cloud, and confused the Egyptian army. 25 He took off their chariot wheels, and they drove them heavily; so that the Egyptians said, "Let's flee from the face of Israel, for Yahweh fights for them against the Egyptians!"
26 Yahweh said to Moses, "Stretch out your hand over the sea, that the waters may come again on the Egyptians, on their chariots, and on their horsemen." 27 Moses stretched out his hand over the sea, and the sea returned to its strength when the morning appeared; and the Egyptians fled against it. Yahweh overthrew the Egyptians in the middle of the sea. 28 The waters returned, and covered the chariots and the horsemen, even all Pharaoh's army that went in after them into the sea. There remained not so much as one of them. 29 But the children of Israel walked on dry land in the middle of the sea, and the waters were a wall to them on their right hand and on their left. 30 Thus Yahweh saved Israel that day out of the hand of the Egyptians; and Israel saw the Egyptians dead on the seashore. 31 Israel saw the great work which Yahweh did to the Egyptians, and the people feared Yahweh; and they believed in Yahweh and in his servant Moses.
1 Then Moses and the children of Israel sang this song to Yahweh, and said,
"I will sing to Yahweh, for he has triumphed gloriously.
He has thrown the horse and his rider into the sea.

Responsorial Psalm: Exodus 15: 1-6, 17-18

1 Then Moses and the children of Israel sang this song to Yahweh, and said,
"I will sing to Yahweh, for he has triumphed gloriously.
He has thrown the horse and his rider into the sea.
2 Yah is my strength and song.
He has become my salvation.
This is my God, and I will praise him;
my father's God, and I will exalt him.
3 Yahweh is a man of war.
Yahweh is his name.
4 He has cast Pharaoh's chariots and his army into the sea.
His chosen captains are sunk in the Red Sea.
5 The deeps cover them.
They went down into the depths like a stone.
6 Your right hand, Yahweh, is glorious in power.

Your right hand, Yahweh, dashes the enemy in pieces.
17 You will bring them in, and plant them in the mountain of your inheritance,
the place, Yahweh, which you have made for yourself to dwell in:
the sanctuary, Lord, which your hands have established.
18 Yahweh will reign forever and ever."

Fourth Reading: Isaiah 54: 5-14

5 For your Maker is your husband; Yahweh of Armies is his name.
The Holy One of Israel is your Redeemer.
He will be called the God of the whole earth.
6 For Yahweh has called you as a wife forsaken and grieved in spirit,
even a wife of youth, when she is cast off," says your God.

7 "For a small moment I have forsaken you,
but I will gather you with great mercies.
8 In overflowing wrath I hid my face from you for a moment,
but with everlasting loving kindness I will have mercy on you," says Yahweh your Redeemer.

9 "For this is like the waters of Noah to me;
for as I have sworn that the waters of Noah will no more go over the earth,
so I have sworn that I will not be angry with you, nor rebuke you.
10 For the mountains may depart,
and the hills be removed,
but my loving kindness will not depart from you,
and my covenant of peace will not be removed,"
says Yahweh who has mercy on you.

11 "You afflicted, tossed with storms, and not comforted,
behold, I will set your stones in beautiful colors,
and lay your foundations with sapphires.
12 I will make your pinnacles of rubies,
your gates of sparkling jewels,
and all your walls of precious stones.
13 All your children will be taught by Yahweh,
and your children's peace will be great.

14 You will be established in righteousness.
You will be far from oppression,
for you will not be afraid,
and far from terror,
for it shall not come near you.

Responsorial Psalm: Psalms 30: 2, 4-6, 11-12

2 Yahweh my God, I cried to you,
and you have healed me.
4 Sing praise to Yahweh, you saints of his.
Give thanks to his holy name.
5 For his anger is but for a moment.
His favor is for a lifetime.
Weeping may stay for the night,
but joy comes in the morning.
6 As for me, I said in my prosperity,
"I shall never be moved."
11 You have turned my mourning into dancing for me.
You have removed my sackcloth, and clothed me with gladness,
12 to the end that my heart may sing praise to you, and not be silent.
Yahweh my God, I will give thanks to you forever!

Fifth Reading: Isaiah 55: 1-11

1 "Hey! Come, everyone who thirsts, to the waters!
Come, he who has no money, buy, and eat!
Yes, come, buy wine and milk without money and without price.
2 Why do you spend money for that which is not bread,
and your labor for that which doesn't satisfy?
Listen diligently to me, and eat that which is good,
and let your soul delight itself in richness.
3 Turn your ear, and come to me.
Hear, and your soul will live.
I will make an everlasting covenant with you, even the sure mercies of David.
4 Behold, I have given him for a witness to the peoples,

a leader and commander to the peoples.
5 Behold, you shall call a nation that you don't know;
and a nation that didn't know you shall run to you,
because of Yahweh your God,
and for the Holy One of Israel;
for he has glorified you."

6 Seek Yahweh while he may be found.
Call on him while he is near.
7 Let the wicked forsake his way,
and the unrighteous man his thoughts.
Let him return to Yahweh, and he will have mercy on him,
to our God, for he will freely pardon.

8 "For my thoughts are not your thoughts,
and your ways are not my ways," says Yahweh.
9 "For as the heavens are higher than the earth,
so are my ways higher than your ways,
and my thoughts than your thoughts.
10 For as the rain comes down and the snow from the sky,
and doesn't return there, but waters the earth,
and makes it grow and bud,
and gives seed to the sower and bread to the eater;
11 so is my word that goes out of my mouth:
it will not return to me void,
but it will accomplish that which I please,
and it will prosper in the thing I sent it to do.

Responsorial Psalm: Isaiah 12: 2-6

2 Behold, God is my salvation. I will trust, and will not be afraid; for Yah, Yahweh, is my strength and song; and he has become my salvation." 3 Therefore with joy you will draw water out of the wells of salvation. 4 In that day you will say, "Give thanks to Yahweh! Call on his name! Declare his doings among the peoples! Proclaim that his name is exalted! 5 Sing to Yahweh, for he has done excellent things! Let this be known in all the earth! 6 Cry aloud and shout, you inhabitant of Zion, for the Holy One of Israel is great among you!"

Sixth Reading: Baruch 3: 9-15, 32 – 4: 4

9 Hear, O Israel, the commandments of life! Give ear to understand wisdom! 10 How is it, O Israel, that you are in your enemies' land, that you have become old in a strange country, that you are defiled with the dead, 11 that you are counted with those who are in Hades? 12 You have forsaken the fountain of wisdom. 13 If you had walked in the way of God, you would have dwelled in peace forever. 14 Learn where there is wisdom, where there is strength, and where there is understanding, that you may also know where there is length of days and life, where there is the light of the eyes and peace. 15 Who has found out her place? Who has come into her treasuries?

32 But he that knows all things knows her, he found her out with his understanding. He who prepared the earth for all time has filled it with four-footed beasts. 33 It is he who sends forth the light, and it goes. He called it, and it obeyed him with fear. 34 The stars shone in their watches, and were glad. When he called them, they said, "Here we are." They shone with gladness to him who made them. 35 This is our God. No other can be compared to him. 36 He has found out all the way of knowledge, and has given it to Jacob his servant and to Israel who is loved by him. 37 Afterward she appeared upon earth, and lived with men.

1 This is the book of God's commandments and the law that endures forever. All those who hold it fast will live, but those who leave it will die. 2 Turn, O Jacob, and take hold of it. Walk toward the shining of its light. 3 Don't give your glory to another, nor the things that are to your advantage to a foreign nation. 4 O Israel, we are happy; for the things that are pleasing to God are made known to us.

Responsorial Psalm: Psalms 19: 8-11

8 Yahweh's precepts are right, rejoicing the heart.
Yahweh's commandment is pure, enlightening the eyes.
9 The fear of Yahweh is clean, enduring forever.
Yahweh's ordinances are true, and righteous altogether.
10 They are more to be desired than gold, yes, than much fine gold,
sweeter also than honey and the extract of the honeycomb.
11 Moreover your servant is warned by them.
In keeping them there is great reward.

Seventh Reading: Ezekiel 36: 16-17a, 18-28

16 Moreover Yahweh's word came to me, saying, 17 "Son of man, when the house of Israel lived in their own land, they defiled it by their ways and by their deeds. 18 Therefore I poured out my wrath on them for the blood which they had poured out on the land, and because they had defiled it with their idols. 19 I scattered them among the nations, and they were dispersed through the countries. I judged them according to their way and according to their deeds. 20 When they came to the nations where they went, they profaned my holy name, in that men said of them, 'These are Yahweh's people, and have left his land.' 21 But I had respect for my holy name, which the house of Israel had profaned among the nations where they went.
22 "Therefore tell the house of Israel, 'The Lord Yahweh says: "I don't do this for your sake, house of Israel, but for my holy name, which you have profaned among the nations where you went. 23 I will sanctify my great name, which has been profaned among the nations, which you have profaned among them. Then the nations will know that I am Yahweh," says the Lord Yahweh, "when I am proven holy in you before their eyes.
24 " ' "For I will take you from among the nations and gather you out of all the countries, and will bring you into your own land. 25 I will sprinkle clean water on you, and you will be clean. I will cleanse you from all your filthiness and from all your idols. 26 I will also give you a new heart, and I will put a new spirit within you. I will take away the stony heart out of your flesh, and I will give you a heart of flesh. 27 I will put my Spirit within you, and cause you to walk in my statutes. You will keep my ordinances and do them. 28 You will dwell in the land that I gave to your fathers. You will be my people, and I will be your God.

Responsorial Psalm: Psalms 42: 3, 5; 43: 3, 4

3 My tears have been my food day and night,
while they continually ask me, "Where is your God?"
5 Why are you in despair, my soul?
Why are you disturbed within me?
Hope in God!
For I shall still praise him for the saving help of his presence.
3 Oh, send out your light and your truth.
Let them lead me.

Let them bring me to your holy hill,
to your tents.
4 Then I will go to the altar of God,
to God, my exceeding joy.
I will praise you on the harp, God, my God.

Epistle Reading: Romans 6: 3-11

3 Or don't you know that all of us who were baptized into Christ Jesus were baptized into his death? 4 We were buried therefore with him through baptism into death, that just as Christ was raised from the dead through the glory of the Father, so we also might walk in newness of life.
5 For if we have become united with him in the likeness of his death, we will also be part of his resurrection; 6 knowing this, that our old man was crucified with him, that the body of sin might be done away with, so that we would no longer be in bondage to sin. 7 For he who has died has been freed from sin. 8 But if we died with Christ, we believe that we will also live with him, 9 knowing that Christ, being raised from the dead, dies no more. Death no longer has dominion over him! 10 For the death that he died, he died to sin one time; but the life that he lives, he lives to God. 11 Thus consider yourselves also to be dead to sin, but alive to God in Christ Jesus our Lord.

Responsorial Psalm: Psalms 118: 1-2, 16-17, 22-23

1 Give thanks to Yahweh, for he is good,
for his loving kindness endures forever.
2 Let Israel now say
that his loving kindness endures forever.
16 The right hand of Yahweh is exalted!
The right hand of Yahweh does valiantly!"
17 I will not die, but live,
and declare Yah's works.
22 The stone which the builders rejected
has become the cornerstone.†
23 This is Yahweh's doing.
It is marvelous in our eyes.

Gospel: Mark 16: 1-7

1 When the Sabbath was past, Mary Magdalene, and Mary the mother of James, and Salome bought spices, that they might come and anoint him. 2 Very early on the first day of the week, they came to the tomb when the sun had risen. 3 They were saying among themselves, "Who will roll away the stone from the door of the tomb for us?" 4 for it was very big. Looking up, they saw that the stone was rolled back.
5 Entering into the tomb, they saw a young man sitting on the right side, dressed in a white robe; and they were amazed. 6 He said to them, "Don't be amazed. You seek Jesus, the Nazarene, who has been crucified. He has risen! He is not here. See the place where they laid him! 7 But go, tell his disciples and Peter, 'He goes before you into Galilee. There you will see him, as he said to you.' "

1. Invite the Holy Spirit into this reading, asking the Author of Scripture to speak to you through His Word
2. Read today's passage as many times as you need, take your time
3. Write down (below) what the Lord is saying to you today
4. Live with this Word in your heart through the day

_____

_____

Sunday, March 31, 2024
EASTER SUNDAY OF THE RESURRECTION OF THE LORD

First Reading: Acts 10: 34a, 37-43

34 Peter opened his mouth and said, 37 you yourselves know what happened, which was proclaimed throughout all Judea, beginning from Galilee, after the baptism which John preached; 38 how God anointed Jesus of Nazareth with the Holy Spirit and with power, who went about doing good and healing all who were oppressed by the devil, for God was with him. 39 We are witnesses of everything he did both in the country of the Jews and in Jerusalem; whom they also‡ killed, hanging him on a tree. 40 God raised him up the third day and gave him to be revealed, 41 not to all the people, but to

witnesses who were chosen before by God, to us, who ate and drank with him after he rose from the dead. 42 He commanded us to preach to the people and to testify that this is he who is appointed by God as the Judge of the living and the dead. 43 All the prophets testify about him, that through his name everyone who believes in him will receive remission of sins."

Responsorial Psalm: Psalms 118: 1-2, 16-17, 22-23

1 Give thanks to Yahweh, for he is good,
for his loving kindness endures forever.
2 Let Israel now say
that his loving kindness endures forever.
16 The right hand of Yahweh is exalted!
The right hand of Yahweh does valiantly!"
17 I will not die, but live,
and declare Yah's works.
22 The stone which the builders rejected
has become the cornerstone.†
23 This is Yahweh's doing.
It is marvelous in our eyes.

Second Reading: Colossians 3: 1-4

1 If then you were raised together with Christ, seek the things that are above, where Christ is, seated on the right hand of God. 2 Set your mind on the things that are above, not on the things that are on the earth. 3 For you died, and your life is hidden with Christ in God. 4 When Christ, our life, is revealed, then you will also be revealed with him in glory.

Gospel: John 20: 1-9

1 Now on the first day of the week, Mary Magdalene went early, while it was still dark, to the tomb, and saw that the stone had been taken away from the tomb. 2 Therefore she ran and came to Simon Peter and to the other disciple whom Jesus loved, and said

to them, "They have taken away the Lord out of the tomb, and we don't know where they have laid him!"

3 Therefore Peter and the other disciple went out, and they went toward the tomb. 4 They both ran together. The other disciple outran Peter and came to the tomb first. 5 Stooping and looking in, he saw the linen cloths lying there; yet he didn't enter in. 6 Then Simon Peter came, following him, and entered into the tomb. He saw the linen cloths lying, 7 and the cloth that had been on his head, not lying with the linen cloths, but rolled up in a place by itself. 8 So then the other disciple who came first to the tomb also entered in, and he saw and believed. 9 For as yet they didn't know the Scripture, that he must rise from the dead.

1. Invite the Holy Spirit into this reading, asking the Author of Scripture to speak to you through His Word
2. Read today's passage as many times as you need, take your time
3. Write down (below) what the Lord is saying to you today
4. Live with this Word in your heart through the day

_____

_____

Sunday, April 7, 2024
SECOND SUNDAY OF EASTER
SUNDAY OF DIVINE MERCY

First Reading: Acts 4: 32-35

32 The multitude of those who believed were of one heart and soul. Not one of them claimed that anything of the things which he possessed was his own, but they had all things in common. 33 With great power, the apostles gave their testimony of the resurrection of the Lord Jesus. Great grace was on them all. 34 For neither was there among them any who lacked, for as many as were owners of lands or houses sold them, and brought the proceeds of the things that were sold, 35 and laid them at the apostles' feet; and distribution was made to each, according as anyone had need.

Responsorial Psalm: Psalms 118: 2-4, 13-15, 22-24

2 Let Israel now say
that his loving kindness endures forever.
3 Let the house of Aaron now say
that his loving kindness endures forever.
4 Now let those who fear Yahweh say
that his loving kindness endures forever.
13 You pushed me back hard, to make me fall,
but Yahweh helped me.
14 Yah is my strength and song.
He has become my salvation.
15 The voice of rejoicing and salvation is in the tents of the righteous.
"The right hand of Yahweh does valiantly.
22 The stone which the builders rejected
has become the cornerstone.†
23 This is Yahweh's doing.
It is marvelous in our eyes.
24 This is the day that Yahweh has made.
We will rejoice and be glad in it!

Second Reading: First John 5: 1-6

1 Whoever believes that Jesus is the Christ has been born of God. Whoever loves the Father also loves the child who is born of him. 2 By this we know that we love the children of God, when we love God and keep his commandments. 3 For this is loving God, that we keep his commandments. His commandments are not grievous. 4 For whatever is born of God overcomes the world. This is the victory that has overcome the world: your faith. 5 Who is he who overcomes the world, but he who believes that Jesus is the Son of God?
6 This is he who came by water and blood, Jesus Christ; not with the water only, but with the water and the blood. It is the Spirit who testifies, because the Spirit is the truth.

Gospel: John 20: 19-31

19 When therefore it was evening on that day, the first day of the week, and when the doors were locked where the disciples were assembled, for fear of the Jews, Jesus came and stood in the middle and said to them, "Peace be to you."
20 When he had said this, he showed them his hands and his side. The disciples therefore were glad when they saw the Lord. 21 Jesus therefore said to them again, "Peace be to you. As the Father has sent me, even so I send you." 22 When he had said this, he breathed on them, and said to them, "Receive the Holy Spirit! 23 If you forgive anyone's sins, they have been forgiven them. If you retain anyone's sins, they have been retained."
24 But Thomas, one of the twelve, called Didymus,§ wasn't with them when Jesus came. 25 The other disciples therefore said to him, "We have seen the Lord!"
But he said to them, "Unless I see in his hands the print of the nails, put my finger into the print of the nails, and put my hand into his side, I will not believe."
26 After eight days, again his disciples were inside and Thomas was with them. Jesus came, the doors being locked, and stood in the middle, and said, "Peace be to you." 27 Then he said to Thomas, "Reach here your finger, and see my hands. Reach here your hand, and put it into my side. Don't be unbelieving, but believing."
28 Thomas answered him, "My Lord and my God!"
29 Jesus said to him, "Because you have seen me,† you have believed. Blessed are those who have not seen and have believed."
30 Therefore Jesus did many other signs in the presence of his disciples, which are not written in this book; 31 but these are written that you may believe that Jesus is the Christ, the Son of God, and that believing you may have life in his name.

1. Invite the Holy Spirit into this reading, asking the Author of Scripture to speak to you through His Word
2. Read today's passage as many times as you need, take your time
3. Write down (below) what the Lord is saying to you today
4. Live with this Word in your heart through the day

_____

_____

Sunday, April 14, 2024
THIRD SUNDAY OF EASTER

First Reading: Acts 3: 13-15, 17-19

13 The God of Abraham, Isaac, and Jacob, the God of our fathers, has glorified his Servant Jesus, whom you delivered up and denied in the presence of Pilate, when he had determined to release him. 14 But you denied the Holy and Righteous One and asked for a murderer to be granted to you, 15 and killed the Prince of life, whom God raised from the dead, to which we are witnesses.
17 "Now, brothers,‡ I know that you did this in ignorance, as did also your rulers. 18 But the things which God announced by the mouth of all his prophets, that Christ should suffer, he thus fulfilled.
19 "Repent therefore, and turn again, that your sins may be blotted out, so that there may come times of refreshing from the presence of the Lord

Responsorial Psalm: Psalms 4: 2, 4, 7-8

2 You sons of men, how long shall my glory be turned into dishonor?
Will you love vanity and seek after falsehood?
4 Stand in awe, and don't sin.
Search your own heart on your bed, and be still.
7 You have put gladness in my heart,
more than when their grain and their new wine are increased.
8 In peace I will both lay myself down and sleep,
for you alone, Yahweh, make me live in safety.

Second Reading: First John 2: 1-5a

1 My little children, I write these things to you so that you may not sin. If anyone sins, we have a Counselor† with the Father, Jesus Christ, the righteous. 2 And he is the atoning sacrifice‡ for our sins, and not for ours only, but also for the whole world. 3 This is how we know that we know him: if we keep his commandments. 4 One who says, "I know him," and doesn't keep his commandments, is a liar, and the truth isn't in him. 5a But God's love has most certainly been perfected in whoever keeps his word.

Gospel: Luke 24: 35-48

35 They related the things that happened along the way, and how he was recognized by them in the breaking of the bread.
36 As they said these things, Jesus himself stood among them, and said to them, "Peace be to you."
37 But they were terrified and filled with fear, and supposed that they had seen a spirit. 38 He said to them, "Why are you troubled? Why do doubts arise in your hearts? 39 See my hands and my feet, that it is truly me. Touch me and see, for a spirit doesn't have flesh and bones, as you see that I have." 40 When he had said this, he showed them his hands and his feet. 41 While they still didn't believe for joy, and wondered, he said to them, "Do you have anything here to eat?"
42 They gave him a piece of a broiled fish and some honeycomb. 43 He took them, and ate in front of them. 44 He said to them, "This is what I told you while I was still with you, that all things which are written in the law of Moses, the prophets, and the psalms concerning me must be fulfilled."
45 Then he opened their minds, that they might understand the Scriptures. 46 He said to them, "Thus it is written, and thus it was necessary for the Christ to suffer and to rise from the dead the third day, 47 and that repentance and remission of sins should be preached in his name to all the nations, beginning at Jerusalem. 48 You are witnesses of these things.

1. Invite the Holy Spirit into this reading, asking the Author of Scripture to speak to you through His Word
2. Read today's passage as many times as you need, take your time
3. Write down (below) what the Lord is saying to you today
4. Live with this Word in your heart through the day

_____
_____

Sunday, April 21, 2024
FOURTH SUNDAY OF EASTER

First Reading: Acts 4: 8-12

8 Then Peter, filled with the Holy Spirit, said to them, "You rulers of the people and elders of Israel, 9 if we are examined today concerning a good deed done to a crippled man, by what means this man has been healed, 10 may it be known to you all, and to all the people of Israel, that in the name of Jesus Christ of Nazareth, whom you crucified, whom God raised from the dead, this man stands here before you whole in him. 11 He is 'the stone which was regarded as worthless by you, the builders, which has become the head of the corner.'* 12 There is salvation in no one else, for there is no other name under heaven that is given among men, by which we must be saved!"

Responsorial Psalm: Psalms 118: 1, 8-9, 21-23, 26, 28, 29

1 Give thanks to Yahweh, for he is good,
for his loving kindness endures forever.
8 It is better to take refuge in Yahweh,
than to put confidence in man.
9 It is better to take refuge in Yahweh,
than to put confidence in princes.
21 I will give thanks to you, for you have answered me,
and have become my salvation.
22 The stone which the builders rejected
has become the cornerstone.†
23 This is Yahweh's doing.
It is marvelous in our eyes.
26 Blessed is he who comes in Yahweh's name!
We have blessed you out of Yahweh's house.
28 You are my God, and I will give thanks to you.
You are my God, I will exalt you.
29 Oh give thanks to Yahweh, for he is good,
for his loving kindness endures forever.

Second Reading: First John 3: 1-2

1 See how great a love the Father has given to us, that we should be called children of God! For this cause the world doesn't know us, because it didn't know him. 2 Beloved, now we are children of God. It is not yet revealed what we will be; but we know that when he is revealed, we will be like him, for we will see him just as he is.

Gospel: John 10: 11-18

11 "I am the good shepherd.* The good shepherd lays down his life for the sheep. 12 He who is a hired hand, and not a shepherd, who doesn't own the sheep, sees the wolf coming, leaves the sheep, and flees. The wolf snatches the sheep and scatters them. 13 The hired hand flees because he is a hired hand and doesn't care for the sheep. 14 I am the good shepherd. I know my own, and I'm known by my own; 15 even as the Father knows me, and I know the Father. I lay down my life for the sheep. 16 I have other sheep which are not of this fold. I must bring them also, and they will hear my voice. They will become one flock with one shepherd. 17 Therefore the Father loves me, because I lay down my life, that I may take it again. 18 No one takes it away from me, but I lay it down by myself. I have power to lay it down, and I have power to take it again. I received this commandment from my Father."

1. Invite the Holy Spirit into this reading, asking the Author of Scripture to speak to you through His Word
2. Read today's passage as many times as you need, take your time
3. Write down (below) what the Lord is saying to you today
4. Live with this Word in your heart through the day

_____

_____

Sunday, April 28, 2024
FIFTH SUNDAY OF EASTER

First Reading: Acts 9: 26-31

26 When Saul had come to Jerusalem, he tried to join himself to the disciples; but they were all afraid of him, not believing that he was a disciple. 27 But Barnabas took him and brought him to the apostles, and declared to them how he had seen the Lord on the way, and that he had spoken to him, and how at Damascus he had preached boldly in the name of Jesus. 28 He was with them entering into† Jerusalem, 29 preaching

boldly in the name of the Lord Jesus.‡ He spoke and disputed against the Hellenists,§ but they were seeking to kill him. 30 When the brothers† knew it, they brought him down to Caesarea and sent him off to Tarsus.

31 So the assemblies throughout all Judea, Galilee, and Samaria had peace and were built up. They were multiplied, walking in the fear of the Lord and in the comfort of the Holy Spirit.

Responsorial Psalm: Psalms 22: 26-28, 30-31

26 The humble shall eat and be satisfied.
They shall praise Yahweh who seek after him.
Let your hearts live forever.
27 All the ends of the earth shall remember and turn to Yahweh.
All the relatives of the nations shall worship before you.
28 For the kingdom is Yahweh's.
He is the ruler over the nations.
30 Posterity shall serve him.
Future generations shall be told about the Lord.
31 They shall come and shall declare his righteousness to a people that shall be born, for he has done it.

Second Reading: First John 3: 18-24

18 My little children, let's not love in word only, or with the tongue only, but in deed and truth. 19 And by this we know that we are of the truth and persuade our hearts before him, 20 because if our heart condemns us, God is greater than our heart, and knows all things. 21 Beloved, if our hearts don't condemn us, we have boldness toward God; 22 so whatever we ask, we receive from him, because we keep his commandments and do the things that are pleasing in his sight. 23 This is his commandment, that we should believe in the name of his Son, Jesus Christ, and love one another, even as he commanded. 24 He who keeps his commandments remains in him, and he in him. By this we know that he remains in us, by the Spirit which he gave us.

Gospel: John 15: 1-8

1 "I am the true vine, and my Father is the farmer. 2 Every branch in me that doesn't bear fruit, he takes away. Every branch that bears fruit, he prunes, that it may bear more fruit. 3 You are already pruned clean because of the word which I have spoken to you. 4 Remain in me, and I in you. As the branch can't bear fruit by itself unless it remains in the vine, so neither can you, unless you remain in me. 5 I am the vine. You are the branches. He who remains in me and I in him bears much fruit, for apart from me you can do nothing. 6 If a man doesn't remain in me, he is thrown out as a branch and is withered; and they gather them, throw them into the fire, and they are burned. 7 If you remain in me, and my words remain in you, you will ask whatever you desire, and it will be done for you.

8 "In this my Father is glorified, that you bear much fruit; and so you will be my disciples.

1. Invite the Holy Spirit into this reading, asking the Author of Scripture to speak to you through His Word
2. Read today's passage as many times as you need, take your time
3. Write down (below) what the Lord is saying to you today
4. Live with this Word in your heart through the day

_____

_____

Sunday, May 5, 2024
SIXTH SUNDAY OF EASTER

First Reading: Acts 10: 25-26, 34-35, 44-48

25 When Peter entered, Cornelius met him, fell down at his feet, and worshiped him. 26 But Peter raised him up, saying, "Stand up! I myself am also a man."
34 Peter opened his mouth and said, "Truly I perceive that God doesn't show favoritism; 35 but in every nation he who fears him and works righteousness is acceptable to him.
44 While Peter was still speaking these words, the Holy Spirit fell on all those who heard the word. 45 They of the circumcision who believed were amazed, as many as

came with Peter, because the gift of the Holy Spirit was also poured out on the Gentiles. 46 For they heard them speaking in other languages and magnifying God.
Then Peter answered, 47 "Can anyone forbid these people from being baptized with water? They have received the Holy Spirit just like us." 48 He commanded them to be baptized in the name of Jesus Christ. Then they asked him to stay some days.

Responsorial Psalm: Psalms 98: 1-4

1 Sing to Yahweh a new song,
for he has done marvelous things!
His right hand and his holy arm have worked salvation for him.
2 Yahweh has made known his salvation.
He has openly shown his righteousness in the sight of the nations.
3 He has remembered his loving kindness and his faithfulness toward the house of Israel.
All the ends of the earth have seen the salvation of our God.
4 Make a joyful noise to Yahweh, all the earth!
Burst out and sing for joy, yes, sing praises!

Second Reading: First John 4: 7-10

7 Beloved, let's love one another, for love is of God; and everyone who loves has been born of God and knows God. 8 He who doesn't love doesn't know God, for God is love. 9 By this God's love was revealed in us, that God has sent his only born† Son into the world that we might live through him. 10 In this is love, not that we loved God, but that he loved us, and sent his Son as the atoning sacrifice‡ for our sins.

Gospel: John 15: 9-17

9 Even as the Father has loved me, I also have loved you. Remain in my love. 10 If you keep my commandments, you will remain in my love, even as I have kept my Father's commandments and remain in his love. 11 I have spoken these things to you, that my joy may remain in you, and that your joy may be made full.
12 "This is my commandment, that you love one another, even as I have loved you. 13 Greater love has no one than this, that someone lay down his life for his friends. 14 You

are my friends if you do whatever I command you. 15 No longer do I call you servants, for the servant doesn't know what his lord does. But I have called you friends, for everything that I heard from my Father, I have made known to you. 16 You didn't choose me, but I chose you and appointed you, that you should go and bear fruit, and that your fruit should remain; that whatever you will ask of the Father in my name, he may give it to you.
17 "I command these things to you, that you may love one another.

1. Invite the Holy Spirit into this reading, asking the Author of Scripture to speak to you through His Word
2. Read today's passage as many times as you need, take your time
3. Write down (below) what the Lord is saying to you today
4. Live with this Word in your heart through the day

_____

_____

Sunday, May 12, 2024
Ascension of the Lord Solemnity (Seventh Sunday of Easter)

First Reading: Acts 1: 1-11

1 The first book I wrote, Theophilus, concerned all that Jesus began both to do and to teach, 2 until the day in which he was received up, after he had given commandment through the Holy Spirit to the apostles whom he had chosen. 3 To these he also showed himself alive after he suffered, by many proofs, appearing to them over a period of forty days and speaking about God's Kingdom. 4 Being assembled together with them, he commanded them, "Don't depart from Jerusalem, but wait for the promise of the Father, which you heard from me. 5 For John indeed baptized in water, but you will be baptized in the Holy Spirit not many days from now."
6 Therefore, when they had come together, they asked him, "Lord, are you now restoring the kingdom to Israel?"
7 He said to them, "It isn't for you to know times or seasons which the Father has set within his own authority. 8 But you will receive power when the Holy Spirit has come

upon you. You will be witnesses to me in Jerusalem, in all Judea and Samaria, and to the uttermost parts of the earth."
9 When he had said these things, as they were looking, he was taken up, and a cloud received him out of their sight. 10 While they were looking steadfastly into the sky as he went, behold,† two men stood by them in white clothing, 11 who also said, "You men of Galilee, why do you stand looking into the sky? This Jesus, who was received up from you into the sky, will come back in the same way as you saw him going into the sky."

Responsorial Psalm: Psalms 47: 2-3, 6-9

2 For Yahweh Most High is awesome.
He is a great King over all the earth.
3 He subdues nations under us,
and peoples under our feet.
6 Sing praises to God! Sing praises!
Sing praises to our King! Sing praises!
7 For God is the King of all the earth.
Sing praises with understanding.
8 God reigns over the nations.
God sits on his holy throne.
9 The princes of the peoples are gathered together,
the people of the God of Abraham.
For the shields of the earth belong to God.
He is greatly exalted!

Second Reading: Ephesians 4: 1-13

1 I therefore, the prisoner in the Lord, beg you to walk worthily of the calling with which you were called, 2 with all lowliness and humility, with patience, bearing with one another in love, 3 being eager to keep the unity of the Spirit in the bond of peace. 4 There is one body and one Spirit, even as you also were called in one hope of your calling, 5 one Lord, one faith, one baptism, 6 one God and Father of all, who is over all and through all and in us all. 7 But to each one of us, the grace was given according to the measure of the gift of Christ. 8 Therefore he says,
"When he ascended on high,
he led captivity captive,

and gave gifts to people."*

9 Now this, "He ascended", what is it but that he also first descended into the lower parts of the earth? 10 He who descended is the one who also ascended far above all the heavens, that he might fill all things.

11 He gave some to be apostles; and some, prophets; and some, evangelists; and some, shepherds† and teachers; 12 for the perfecting of the saints, to the work of serving, to the building up of the body of Christ, 13 until we all attain to the unity of the faith and of the knowledge of the Son of God, to a full grown man, to the measure of the stature of the fullness of Christ

Gospel: Mark 16: 15-20

15 He said to them, "Go into all the world and preach the Good News to the whole creation. 16 He who believes and is baptized will be saved; but he who disbelieves will be condemned. 17 These signs will accompany those who believe: in my name they will cast out demons; they will speak with new languages; 18 they will take up serpents; and if they drink any deadly thing, it will in no way hurt them; they will lay hands on the sick, and they will recover."

19 So then the Lord,† after he had spoken to them, was received up into heaven and sat down at the right hand of God. 20 They went out and preached everywhere, the Lord working with them and confirming the word by the signs that followed. Amen.

1. Invite the Holy Spirit into this reading, asking the Author of Scripture to speak to you through His Word
2. Read today's passage as many times as you need, take your time
3. Write down (below) what the Lord is saying to you today
4. Live with this Word in your heart through the day

_____

_____

Sunday, May 19, 2024
PENTECOST SUNDAY

First Reading: Acts 2: 1-11

1 Now when the day of Pentecost had come, they were all with one accord in one place. 2 Suddenly there came from the sky a sound like the rushing of a mighty wind, and it filled all the house where they were sitting. 3 Tongues like fire appeared and were distributed to them, and one sat on each of them. 4 They were all filled with the Holy Spirit and began to speak with other languages, as the Spirit gave them the ability to speak.

5 Now there were dwelling in Jerusalem Jews, devout men, from every nation under the sky. 6 When this sound was heard, the multitude came together and were bewildered, because everyone heard them speaking in his own language. 7 They were all amazed and marveled, saying to one another, "Behold, aren't all these who speak Galileans? 8 How do we hear, everyone in our own native language? 9 Parthians, Medes, Elamites, and people from Mesopotamia, Judea, Cappadocia, Pontus, Asia, 10 Phrygia, Pamphylia, Egypt, the parts of Libya around Cyrene, visitors from Rome, both Jews and proselytes, 11 Cretans and Arabians—we hear them speaking in our languages the mighty works of God!"

Responsorial Psalm: Psalms 104: 1, 24, 29-31, 34

1 Bless Yahweh, my soul.
Yahweh, my God, you are very great.
You are clothed with honor and majesty.
24 Yahweh, how many are your works!
In wisdom, you have made them all.
The earth is full of your riches.
29 You hide your face; they are troubled.
You take away their breath; they die and return to the dust.
30 You send out your Spirit and they are created.
You renew the face of the ground.
31 Let Yahweh's glory endure forever.
Let Yahweh rejoice in his works.
34 Let my meditation be sweet to him.
I will rejoice in Yahweh.

Second Reading: First Corinthians 12: 3b-7, 12-13

3b No one can say, "Jesus is Lord," but by the Holy Spirit. 4 Now there are various kinds of gifts, but the same Spirit. 5 There are various kinds of service, and the same Lord. 6 There are various kinds of workings, but the same God who works all things in all. 7 But to each one is given the manifestation of the Spirit for the profit of all.

12 For as the body is one and has many members, and all the members of the body, being many, are one body; so also is Christ. 13 For in one Spirit we were all baptized into one body, whether Jews or Greeks, whether bond or free; and were all given to drink into one Spirit.

Gospel: John 20: 19-23

19 When therefore it was evening on that day, the first day of the week, and when the doors were locked where the disciples were assembled, for fear of the Jews, Jesus came and stood in the middle and said to them, "Peace be to you."

20 When he had said this, he showed them his hands and his side. The disciples therefore were glad when they saw the Lord. 21 Jesus therefore said to them again, "Peace be to you. As the Father has sent me, even so I send you." 22 When he had said this, he breathed on them, and said to them, "Receive the Holy Spirit! 23 If you forgive anyone's sins, they have been forgiven them. If you retain anyone's sins, they have been retained."

1. Invite the Holy Spirit into this reading, asking the Author of Scripture to speak to you through His Word
2. Read today's passage as many times as you need, take your time
3. Write down (below) what the Lord is saying to you today
4. Live with this Word in your heart through the day

_____

_____

Sunday, May 26, 2024
THE MOST HOLY TRINITY

First Reading: Deuteronomy 4: 32-34, 39-40

32 For ask now of the days that are past, which were before you, since the day that God created man on the earth, and from the one end of the sky to the other, whether there has been anything as great as this thing is, or has been heard like it? 33 Did a people ever hear the voice of God speaking out of the middle of the fire, as you have heard, and live? 34 Or has God tried to go and take a nation for himself from among another nation, by trials, by signs, by wonders, by war, by a mighty hand, by an outstretched arm, and by great terrors, according to all that Yahweh your God did for you in Egypt before your eyes?

39 Know therefore today, and take it to heart, that Yahweh himself is God in heaven above and on the earth beneath. There is no one else. 40 You shall keep his statutes and his commandments which I command you today, that it may go well with you and with your children after you, and that you may prolong your days in the land which Yahweh your God gives you for all time.

Responsorial Psalm: Psalms 33: 4-6, 9, 18-20, 22

4 For Yahweh's word is right.
All his work is done in faithfulness.
5 He loves righteousness and justice.
The earth is full of the loving kindness of Yahweh.
6 By Yahweh's word, the heavens were made:
all their army by the breath of his mouth.
9 For he spoke, and it was done.
He commanded, and it stood firm.
18 Behold, Yahweh's eye is on those who fear him,
on those who hope in his loving kindness,
19 to deliver their soul from death,
to keep them alive in famine.
20 Our soul has waited for Yahweh.
He is our help and our shield.
22 Let your loving kindness be on us, Yahweh,
since we have hoped in you.

Second Reading: Romans 8: 14-17

14 For as many as are led by the Spirit of God, these are children of God. 15 For you didn't receive the spirit of bondage again to fear, but you received the Spirit of adoption, by whom we cry, "Abba!‡ Father!"

16 The Spirit himself testifies with our spirit that we are children of God; 17 and if children, then heirs—heirs of God and joint heirs with Christ, if indeed we suffer with him, that we may also be glorified with him.

Gospel: Matthew 28: 16-20

16 But the eleven disciples went into Galilee, to the mountain where Jesus had sent them. 17 When they saw him, they bowed down to him; but some doubted. 18 Jesus came to them and spoke to them, saying, "All authority has been given to me in heaven and on earth. 19 Go‡ and make disciples of all nations, baptizing them in the name of the Father and of the Son and of the Holy Spirit, 20 teaching them to observe all things that I commanded you. Behold, I am with you always, even to the end of the age." Amen.

1. Invite the Holy Spirit into this reading, asking the Author of Scripture to speak to you through His Word
2. Read today's passage as many times as you need, take your time
3. Write down (below) what the Lord is saying to you today
4. Live with this Word in your heart through the day

_____

_____

Sunday, June 2, 2024
THE MOST HOLY BODY AND BLOOD OF CHRIST
(Corpus Christi)

First Reading: Exodus 24: 3-8

3 Moses came and told the people all Yahweh's words, and all the ordinances; and all the people answered with one voice, and said, "All the words which Yahweh has spoken will we do."

4 Moses wrote all Yahweh's words, then rose up early in the morning and built an altar at the base of the mountain, with twelve pillars for the twelve tribes of Israel. 5 He sent young men of the children of Israel, who offered burnt offerings and sacrificed peace offerings of cattle to Yahweh. 6 Moses took half of the blood and put it in basins, and half of the blood he sprinkled on the altar. 7 He took the book of the covenant and read it in the hearing of the people, and they said, "We will do all that Yahweh has said, and be obedient."

8 Moses took the blood, and sprinkled it on the people, and said, "Look, this is the blood of the covenant, which Yahweh has made with you concerning all these words."

Responsorial Psalm: Psalms 116: 12-13, 15-18

12 What will I give to Yahweh for all his benefits toward me?
13 I will take the cup of salvation, and call on Yahweh's name.
15 Precious in Yahweh's sight is the death of his saints.
16 Yahweh, truly I am your servant.
I am your servant, the son of your servant girl.
You have freed me from my chains.
17 I will offer to you the sacrifice of thanksgiving,
and will call on Yahweh's name.
18 I will pay my vows to Yahweh,
yes, in the presence of all his people,

Second Reading: Hebrews 9: 11-15

11 But Christ having come as a high priest of the coming good things, through the greater and more perfect tabernacle, not made with hands, that is to say, not of this creation, 12 nor yet through the blood of goats and calves, but through his own blood, entered in once for all into the Holy Place, having obtained eternal redemption. 13 For if the blood of goats and bulls, and the ashes of a heifer sprinkling those who have been defiled, sanctify to the cleanness of the flesh, 14 how much more will the blood of Christ, who through the eternal Spirit offered himself without defect to God, cleanse your conscience from dead works to serve the living God? 15 For this reason he is the

mediator of a new covenant, since a death has occurred for the redemption of the transgressions that were under the first covenant, that those who have been called may receive the promise of the eternal inheritance.

Gospel: Mark 14: 12-16, 22-26

12 On the first day of unleavened bread, when they sacrificed the Passover, his disciples asked him, "Where do you want us to go and prepare that you may eat the Passover?"
13 He sent two of his disciples and said to them, "Go into the city, and there a man carrying a pitcher of water will meet you. Follow him, 14 and wherever he enters in, tell the master of the house, 'The Teacher says, "Where is the guest room, where I may eat the Passover with my disciples?"' 15 He will himself show you a large upper room furnished and ready. Get ready for us there."
16 His disciples went out, and came into the city, and found things as he had said to them, and they prepared the Passover.
22 As they were eating, Jesus took bread, and when he had blessed it, he broke it and gave to them, and said, "Take, eat. This is my body."
23 He took the cup, and when he had given thanks, he gave to them. They all drank of it. 24 He said to them, "This is my blood of the new covenant, which is poured out for many. 25 Most certainly I tell you, I will no more drink of the fruit of the vine until that day when I drink it anew in God's Kingdom." 26 When they had sung a hymn, they went out to the Mount of Olives.

1. Invite the Holy Spirit into this reading, asking the Author of Scripture to speak to you through His Word
2. Read today's passage as many times as you need, take your time
3. Write down (below) what the Lord is saying to you today
4. Live with this Word in your heart through the day

_____

_____

Sunday, June 9, 2024
TENTH SUNDAY IN ORDINARY TIME

First Reading: Genesis 3: 9-15

9 Yahweh God called to the man, and said to him, "Where are you?"
10 The man said, "I heard your voice in the garden, and I was afraid, because I was naked; so I hid myself."
11 God said, "Who told you that you were naked? Have you eaten from the tree that I commanded you not to eat from?"
12 The man said, "The woman whom you gave to be with me, she gave me fruit from the tree, and I ate it."
13 Yahweh God said to the woman, "What have you done?"
The woman said, "The serpent deceived me, and I ate."
14 Yahweh God said to the serpent,
"Because you have done this,
you are cursed above all livestock,
and above every animal of the field.
You shall go on your belly
and you shall eat dust all the days of your life.
15 I will put hostility between you and the woman,
and between your offspring and her offspring.
He will bruise your head,
and you will bruise his heel."

Responsorial Psalm: Psalms 130: 1-8

1 Out of the depths I have cried to you, Yahweh.
2 Lord, hear my voice.
Let your ears be attentive to the voice of my petitions.
3 If you, Yah, kept a record of sins,
Lord, who could stand?
4 But there is forgiveness with you,
therefore you are feared.
5 I wait for Yahweh.
My soul waits.
I hope in his word.
6 My soul longs for the Lord more than watchmen long for the morning,
more than watchmen for the morning.

7 Israel, hope in Yahweh,
for there is loving kindness with Yahweh.
Abundant redemption is with him.
8 He will redeem Israel from all their sins.

Second Reading: Second Corinthians 4: 13 – 5:1

13 But having the same spirit of faith, according to that which is written, "I believed, and therefore I spoke."* We also believe, and therefore we also speak, 14 knowing that he who raised the Lord Jesus will raise us also with Jesus, and will present us with you. 15 For all things are for your sakes, that the grace, being multiplied through the many, may cause the thanksgiving to abound to the glory of God.
16 Therefore we don't faint, but though our outward person is decaying, yet our inward person is renewed day by day. 17 For our light affliction, which is for the moment, works for us more and more exceedingly an eternal weight of glory, 18 while we don't look at the things which are seen, but at the things which are not seen. For the things which are seen are temporal, but the things which are not seen are eternal.
1 For we know that if the earthly house of our tent is dissolved, we have a building from God, a house not made with hands, eternal, in the heavens.

Gospel: Mark 3: 20-35

20 The multitude came together again, so that they could not so much as eat bread. 21 When his friends heard it, they went out to seize him; for they said, "He is insane." 22 The scribes who came down from Jerusalem said, "He has Beelzebul," and, "By the prince of the demons he casts out the demons."
23 He summoned them and said to them in parables, "How can Satan cast out Satan? 24 If a kingdom is divided against itself, that kingdom cannot stand. 25 If a house is divided against itself, that house cannot stand. 26 If Satan has risen up against himself, and is divided, he can't stand, but has an end. 27 But no one can enter into the house of the strong man to plunder unless he first binds the strong man; then he will plunder his house.
28 "Most certainly I tell you, all sins of the descendants of man will be forgiven, including their blasphemies with which they may blaspheme; 29 but whoever may blaspheme against the Holy Spirit never has forgiveness, but is subject to eternal condemnation."† 30 —because they said, "He has an unclean spirit."

31 His mother and his brothers came, and standing outside, they sent to him, calling him. 32 A multitude was sitting around him, and they told him, "Behold, your mother, your brothers, and your sisters‡ are outside looking for you."
33 He answered them, "Who are my mother and my brothers?" 34 Looking around at those who sat around him, he said, "Behold, my mother and my brothers! 35 For whoever does the will of God is my brother, my sister, and mother."

1. Invite the Holy Spirit into this reading, asking the Author of Scripture to speak to you through His Word
2. Read today's passage as many times as you need, take your time
3. Write down (below) what the Lord is saying to you today
4. Live with this Word in your heart through the day

_____

_____

Sunday, June 16, 2024
ELEVENTH SUNDAY IN ORDINARY TIME

First Reading: Ezekiel 17: 22-24

22 "The Lord Yahweh says: 'I will also take some of the lofty top of the cedar, and will plant it. I will crop off from the topmost of its young twigs a tender one, and I will plant it on a high and lofty mountain. 23 I will plant it in the mountain of the height of Israel; and it will produce boughs, and bear fruit, and be a good cedar. Birds of every kind will dwell in the shade of its branches. 24 All the trees of the field will know that I, Yahweh, have brought down the high tree, have exalted the low tree, have dried up the green tree, and have made the dry tree flourish.
" 'I, Yahweh, have spoken and have done it.' "

Responsorial Psalm: Psalms 92: 2-3, 13-15

2 to proclaim your loving kindness in the morning,
and your faithfulness every night,

3 with the ten-stringed lute, with the harp,
and with the melody of the lyre.
13 They are planted in Yahweh's house.
They will flourish in our God's courts.
14 They will still produce fruit in old age.
They will be full of sap and green,
15 to show that Yahweh is upright.
He is my rock,
and there is no unrighteousness in him.

Second Reading: Second Corinthians 5: 6-10

6 Therefore we are always confident and know that while we are at home in the body, we are absent from the Lord; 7 for we walk by faith, not by sight. 8 We are courageous, I say, and are willing rather to be absent from the body and to be at home with the Lord. 9 Therefore also we make it our aim, whether at home or absent, to be well pleasing to him. 10 For we must all be revealed before the judgment seat of Christ that each one may receive the things in the body according to what he has done, whether good or bad.

Gospel: Mark 4: 26-34

26 He said, "God's Kingdom is as if a man should cast seed on the earth, 27 and should sleep and rise night and day, and the seed should spring up and grow, though he doesn't know how. 28 For the earth bears fruit by itself: first the blade, then the ear, then the full grain in the ear. 29 But when the fruit is ripe, immediately he puts in the sickle, because the harvest has come."
30 He said, "How will we liken God's Kingdom? Or with what parable will we illustrate it? 31 It's like a grain of mustard seed, which, when it is sown in the earth, though it is less than all the seeds that are on the earth, 32 yet when it is sown, grows up and becomes greater than all the herbs, and puts out great branches, so that the birds of the sky can lodge under its shadow."
33 With many such parables he spoke the word to them, as they were able to hear it. 34 Without a parable he didn't speak to them; but privately to his own disciples he explained everything.

1. Invite the Holy Spirit into this reading, asking the Author of Scripture to speak to you through His Word
2. Read today's passage as many times as you need, take your time
3. Write down (below) what the Lord is saying to you today
4. Live with this Word in your heart through the day

_____
_____

Sunday, June 23, 2024
TWELFTH SUNDAY IN ORDINARY TIME

First Reading: Job 38: 1, 8-11

1 Then Yahweh answered Job out of the whirlwind,
8 "Or who shut up the sea with doors,
when it broke out of the womb,
9 when I made clouds its garment,
and wrapped it in thick darkness,
10 marked out for it my bound,
set bars and doors,
11 and said, 'You may come here, but no further.
Your proud waves shall be stopped here'?

Responsorial Psalm: Psalms 107: 23-26, 28-31

23 Those who go down to the sea in ships,
who do business in great waters,
24 these see Yahweh's deeds,
and his wonders in the deep.
25 For he commands, and raises the stormy wind,
which lifts up its waves.
26 They mount up to the sky; they go down again to the depths.
Their soul melts away because of trouble.

28 Then they cry to Yahweh in their trouble,
and he brings them out of their distress.
29 He makes the storm a calm,
so that its waves are still.
30 Then they are glad because it is calm,
so he brings them to their desired haven.
31 Let them praise Yahweh for his loving kindness,
for his wonderful deeds for the children of men!

Second Reading: Second Corinthians 5: 14-17

14 For the love of Christ compels us; because we judge thus: that one died for all, therefore all died. 15 He died for all, that those who live should no longer live to themselves, but to him who for their sakes died and rose again.
16 Therefore we know no one according to the flesh from now on. Even though we have known Christ according to the flesh, yet now we know him so no more. 17 Therefore if anyone is in Christ, he is a new creation. The old things have passed away. Behold,† all things have become new.

Gospel: Mark 4: 35-41

35 On that day, when evening had come, he said to them, "Let's go over to the other side." 36 Leaving the multitude, they took him with them, even as he was, in the boat. Other small boats were also with him. 37 A big wind storm arose, and the waves beat into the boat, so much that the boat was already filled. 38 He himself was in the stern, asleep on the cushion; and they woke him up and asked him, "Teacher, don't you care that we are dying?"
39 He awoke and rebuked the wind, and said to the sea, "Peace! Be still!" The wind ceased and there was a great calm. 40 He said to them, "Why are you so afraid? How is it that you have no faith?"
41 They were greatly afraid and said to one another, "Who then is this, that even the wind and the sea obey him?"

1. Invite the Holy Spirit into this reading, asking the Author of Scripture to speak to you through His Word
2. Read today's passage as many times as you need, take your time

3. Write down (below) what the Lord is saying to you today
4. Live with this Word in your heart through the day

_____
_____

Sunday, June 30, 2024
THIRTEENTH SUNDAY IN ORDINARY TIME

First Reading: Wisdom 1: 13-15; 2: 23-24

13 because God didn't make death,
neither does he delight when the living perish.
14 For he created all things that they might have being.
The generative powers of the world are wholesome,
and there is no poison of destruction in them,
nor has Hades‡ royal dominion upon earth;
15 for righteousness is immortal,
23 Because God created man for incorruption,
and made him an image of his own everlastingness;
24 but death entered into the world by the envy of the devil,
and those who belong to him experience it.

Responsorial Psalm: Psalms 30: 2, 4-6, 11- 12

2 Yahweh my God, I cried to you,
and you have healed me.
4 Sing praise to Yahweh, you saints of his.
Give thanks to his holy name.
5 For his anger is but for a moment.
His favor is for a lifetime.
Weeping may stay for the night,
but joy comes in the morning.
6 As for me, I said in my prosperity,

"I shall never be moved."
11 You have turned my mourning into dancing for me.
You have removed my sackcloth, and clothed me with gladness,
12 to the end that my heart may sing praise to you, and not be silent.
Yahweh my God, I will give thanks to you forever!

Second Reading: Second Corinthians 8: 7, 9, 13-15

7 But as you abound in everything—in faith, utterance, knowledge, all earnestness, and in your love to us—see that you also abound in this grace.
9 For you know the grace of our Lord Jesus Christ, that though he was rich, yet for your sakes he became poor, that you through his poverty might become rich.
13 For this is not that others may be eased and you distressed, 14 but for equality. Your abundance at this present time supplies their lack, that their abundance also may become a supply for your lack, that there may be equality. 15 As it is written, "He who gathered much had nothing left over, and he who gathered little had no lack."

Gospel: Mark 5: 21-43

21 When Jesus had crossed back over in the boat to the other side, a great multitude was gathered to him; and he was by the sea. 22 Behold, one of the rulers of the synagogue, Jairus by name, came; and seeing him, he fell at his feet 23 and begged him much, saying, "My little daughter is at the point of death. Please come and lay your hands on her, that she may be made healthy, and live."
24 He went with him, and a great multitude followed him, and they pressed upon him on all sides. 25 A certain woman who had a discharge of blood for twelve years, 26 and had suffered many things by many physicians, and had spent all that she had, and was no better, but rather grew worse, 27 having heard the things concerning Jesus, came up behind him in the crowd and touched his clothes. 28 For she said, "If I just touch his clothes, I will be made well." 29 Immediately the flow of her blood was dried up, and she felt in her body that she was healed of her affliction.
30 Immediately Jesus, perceiving in himself that the power had gone out from him, turned around in the crowd and asked, "Who touched my clothes?"
31 His disciples said to him, "You see the multitude pressing against you, and you say, 'Who touched me?' "

32 He looked around to see her who had done this thing. 33 But the woman, fearing and trembling, knowing what had been done to her, came and fell down before him, and told him all the truth.

34 He said to her, "Daughter, your faith has made you well. Go in peace, and be cured of your disease."

35 While he was still speaking, people came from the synagogue ruler's house, saying, "Your daughter is dead. Why bother the Teacher any more?"

36 But Jesus, when he heard the message spoken, immediately said to the ruler of the synagogue, "Don't be afraid, only believe." 37 He allowed no one to follow him except Peter, James, and John the brother of James. 38 He came to the synagogue ruler's house, and he saw an uproar, weeping, and great wailing. 39 When he had entered in, he said to them, "Why do you make an uproar and weep? The child is not dead, but is asleep."

40 They ridiculed him. But he, having put them all out, took the father of the child, her mother, and those who were with him, and went in where the child was lying. 41 Taking the child by the hand, he said to her, "Talitha cumi!" which means, being interpreted, "Girl, I tell you, get up!" 42 Immediately the girl rose up and walked, for she was twelve years old. They were amazed with great amazement. 43 He strictly ordered them that no one should know this, and commanded that something should be given to her to eat.

1. Invite the Holy Spirit into this reading, asking the Author of Scripture to speak to you through His Word
2. Read today's passage as many times as you need, take your time
3. Write down (below) what the Lord is saying to you today
4. Live with this Word in your heart through the day

_____

_____

Sunday, July 7, 2024
FOURTEENTH SUNDAY IN ORDINARY TIME

First Reading: Ezekiel 2: 2-5

2 The Spirit entered into me when he spoke to me, and set me on my feet; and I heard him who spoke to me.

3 He said to me, "Son of man, I send you to the children of Israel, to a nation of rebels who have rebelled against me. They and their fathers have transgressed against me even to this very day. 4 The children are impudent and stiff-hearted. I am sending you to them, and you shall tell them, 'This is what the Lord† Yahweh says.' 5 They, whether they will hear, or whether they will refuse—for they are a rebellious house—yet they will know that there has been a prophet among them.

Responsorial Psalm: Psalms 123: 1-4

1 I lift up my eyes to you,
you who sit in the heavens.
2 Behold, as the eyes of servants look to the hand of their master,
as the eyes of a maid to the hand of her mistress,
so our eyes look to Yahweh, our God,
until he has mercy on us.
3 Have mercy on us, Yahweh, have mercy on us,
for we have endured much contempt.
4 Our soul is exceedingly filled with the scoffing of those who are at ease,
with the contempt of the proud.

Second Reading: Second Corinthians 12: 7-10

7 By reason of the exceeding greatness of the revelations, that I should not be exalted excessively, a thorn in the flesh was given to me: a messenger of Satan to torment me, that I should not be exalted excessively. 8 Concerning this thing, I begged the Lord three times that it might depart from me. 9 He has said to me, "My grace is sufficient for you, for my power is made perfect in weakness." Most gladly therefore I will rather glory in my weaknesses, that the power of Christ may rest on me.

10 Therefore I take pleasure in weaknesses, in injuries, in necessities, in persecutions, and in distresses, for Christ's sake. For when I am weak, then am I strong.

Gospel: Mark 6: 1-6

1 He went out from there. He came into his own country, and his disciples followed him. 2 When the Sabbath had come, he began to teach in the synagogue, and many hearing him were astonished, saying, "Where did this man get these things?" and, "What is the wisdom that is given to this man, that such mighty works come about by his hands? 3 Isn't this the carpenter, the son of Mary and brother of James, Joses, Judah, and Simon? Aren't his sisters here with us?" So they were offended at him.
4 Jesus said to them, "A prophet is not without honor, except in his own country, and among his own relatives, and in his own house." 5 He could do no mighty work there, except that he laid his hands on a few sick people and healed them. 6 He marveled because of their unbelief.

1. Invite the Holy Spirit into this reading, asking the Author of Scripture to speak to you through His Word
2. Read today's passage as many times as you need, take your time
3. Write down (below) what the Lord is saying to you today
4. Live with this Word in your heart through the day

_____

_____

Sunday, July 14, 2024
FIFTEENTH SUNDAY IN ORDINARY TIME

First Reading: Amos 7: 12-15

12 Amaziah also said to Amos, "You seer, go, flee away into the land of Judah, and there eat bread, and prophesy there, 13 but don't prophesy again any more at Bethel; for it is the king's sanctuary, and it is a royal house!"
14 Then Amos answered Amaziah, "I was no prophet, neither was I a prophet's son, but I was a herdsman, and a farmer of sycamore figs; 15 and Yahweh took me from following the flock, and Yahweh said to me, 'Go, prophesy to my people Israel.'

Responsorial Psalm: Psalms 85: 9-13

9 Surely his salvation is near those who fear him,
that glory may dwell in our land.
10 Mercy and truth meet together.
Righteousness and peace have kissed each other.
11 Truth springs out of the earth.
Righteousness has looked down from heaven.
12 Yes, Yahweh will give that which is good.
Our land will yield its increase.
13 Righteousness goes before him,
and prepares the way for his steps.

Second Reading: Ephesians 1: 3-14

3 Blessed be the God and Father of our Lord Jesus Christ, who has blessed us with every spiritual blessing in the heavenly places in Christ, 4 even as he chose us in him before the foundation of the world, that we would be holy and without defect before him in love, 5 having predestined us for adoption as children through Jesus Christ to himself, according to the good pleasure of his desire, 6 to the praise of the glory of his grace, by which he freely gave us favor in the Beloved. 7 In him we have our redemption through his blood, the forgiveness of our trespasses, according to the riches of his grace 8 which he made to abound toward us in all wisdom and prudence, 9 making known to us the mystery of his will, according to his good pleasure which he purposed in him 10 to an administration of the fullness of the times, to sum up all things in Christ, the things in the heavens and the things on the earth, in him. 11 We were also assigned an inheritance in him, having been foreordained according to the purpose of him who does all things after the counsel of his will, 12 to the end that we should be to the praise of his glory, we who had before hoped in Christ. 13 In him you also, having heard the word of the truth, the Good News of your salvation—in whom, having also believed, you were sealed with the promised Holy Spirit, 14 who is a pledge of our inheritance, to the redemption of God's own possession, to the praise of his glory.

Gospel: Mark 6: 7-13

7 He called to himself the twelve, and began to send them out two by two; and he gave them authority over the unclean spirits. 8 He commanded them that they should take nothing for their journey, except a staff only: no bread, no wallet, no money in their

purse, 9 but to wear sandals, and not put on two tunics. 10 He said to them, "Wherever you enter into a house, stay there until you depart from there. 11 Whoever will not receive you nor hear you, as you depart from there, shake off the dust that is under your feet for a testimony against them. Assuredly, I tell you, it will be more tolerable for Sodom and Gomorrah in the day of judgment than for that city!"
12 They went out and preached that people should repent. 13 They cast out many demons, and anointed many with oil who were sick and healed them.

1. Invite the Holy Spirit into this reading, asking the Author of Scripture to speak to you through His Word
2. Read today's passage as many times as you need, take your time
3. Write down (below) what the Lord is saying to you today
4. Live with this Word in your heart through the day

_____

_____

Sunday, July 21, 2024
SIXTEENTH SUNDAY IN ORDINARY TIME

First Reading: Jeremiah 23: 1-6

1 "Woe to the shepherds who destroy and scatter the sheep of my pasture!" says Yahweh. 2 Therefore Yahweh, the God of Israel, says against the shepherds who feed my people: "You have scattered my flock, driven them away, and have not visited them. Behold, I will visit on you the evil of your doings," says Yahweh. 3 "I will gather the remnant of my flock out of all the countries where I have driven them, and will bring them again to their folds; and they will be fruitful and multiply. 4 I will set up shepherds over them who will feed them. They will no longer be afraid or dismayed, neither will any be lacking," says Yahweh.
5 "Behold, the days come," says Yahweh,
"that I will raise to David a righteous Branch;
and he will reign as king and deal wisely,
and will execute justice and righteousness in the land.
6 In his days Judah will be saved,

and Israel will dwell safely.
This is his name by which he will be called:
Yahweh our righteousness.

Responsorial Psalm: Psalms 23: 1-6

1 Yahweh is my shepherd;
I shall lack nothing.
2 He makes me lie down in green pastures.
He leads me beside still waters.
3 He restores my soul.
He guides me in the paths of righteousness for his name's sake.
4 Even though I walk through the valley of the shadow of death,
I will fear no evil, for you are with me.
Your rod and your staff,
they comfort me.
5 You prepare a table before me
in the presence of my enemies.
You anoint my head with oil.
My cup runs over.
6 Surely goodness and loving kindness shall follow me all the days of my life,
and I will dwell in Yahweh's house forever.

Second Reading: Ephesians 2: 13-18

13 But now in Christ Jesus you who once were far off are made near in the blood of Christ. 14 For he is our peace, who made both one, and broke down the middle wall of separation, 15 having abolished in his flesh the hostility, the law of commandments contained in ordinances, that he might create in himself one new man of the two, making peace, 16 and might reconcile them both in one body to God through the cross, having killed the hostility through it. 17 He came and preached peace to you who were far off and to those who were near. 18 For through him we both have our access in one Spirit to the Father.

Gospel: Mark 6: 30-34

30 The apostles gathered themselves together to Jesus, and they told him all things, whatever they had done, and whatever they had taught. 31 He said to them, "Come away into a deserted place, and rest awhile." For there were many coming and going, and they had no leisure so much as to eat. 32 They went away in the boat to a deserted place by themselves. 33 They† saw them going, and many recognized him and ran there on foot from all the cities. They arrived before them and came together to him. 34 Jesus came out, saw a great multitude, and he had compassion on them because they were like sheep without a shepherd; and he began to teach them many things.

1. Invite the Holy Spirit into this reading, asking the Author of Scripture to speak to you through His Word
2. Read today's passage as many times as you need, take your time
3. Write down (below) what the Lord is saying to you today
4. Live with this Word in your heart through the day

_____

_____

Sunday, July 28, 2024
SEVENTEENTH SUNDAY IN ORDINARY TIME

First Reading: Second Kings 4: 42-44

42 A man from Baal Shalishah came, and brought the man of God some bread of the first fruits: twenty loaves of barley and fresh ears of grain in his sack. Elisha said, "Give to the people, that they may eat."
43 His servant said, "What, should I set this before a hundred men?"
But he said, "Give it to the people, that they may eat; for Yahweh says, 'They will eat, and will have some left over.' "
44 So he set it before them and they ate and had some left over, according to Yahweh's word.

Responsorial Psalm: Psalms 145: 10-11, 15-18

10 All your works will give thanks to you, Yahweh.
Your saints will extol you.
11 They will speak of the glory of your kingdom,
and talk about your power,
15 The eyes of all wait for you.
You give them their food in due season.
16 You open your hand,
and satisfy the desire of every living thing.
17 Yahweh is righteous in all his ways,
and gracious in all his works.
18 Yahweh is near to all those who call on him,
to all who call on him in truth.

Second Reading: Ephesians 4: 1-6

1 I therefore, the prisoner in the Lord, beg you to walk worthily of the calling with which you were called, 2 with all lowliness and humility, with patience, bearing with one another in love, 3 being eager to keep the unity of the Spirit in the bond of peace. 4 There is one body and one Spirit, even as you also were called in one hope of your calling, 5 one Lord, one faith, one baptism, 6 one God and Father of all, who is over all and through all and in us all.

Gospel: John 6: 1-15

1 After these things, Jesus went away to the other side of the sea of Galilee, which is also called the Sea of Tiberias. 2 A great multitude followed him, because they saw his signs which he did on those who were sick. 3 Jesus went up into the mountain, and he sat there with his disciples. 4 Now the Passover, the feast of the Jews, was at hand. 5 Jesus therefore, lifting up his eyes and seeing that a great multitude was coming to him, said to Philip, "Where are we to buy bread, that these may eat?" 6 He said this to test him, for he himself knew what he would do.
7 Philip answered him, "Two hundred denarii† worth of bread is not sufficient for them, that every one of them may receive a little."
8 One of his disciples, Andrew, Simon Peter's brother, said to him, 9 "There is a boy here who has five barley loaves and two fish, but what are these among so many?"

10 Jesus said, "Have the people sit down." Now there was much grass in that place. So the men sat down, in number about five thousand. 11 Jesus took the loaves, and having given thanks, he distributed to the disciples, and the disciples to those who were sitting down, likewise also of the fish as much as they desired. 12 When they were filled, he said to his disciples, "Gather up the broken pieces which are left over, that nothing be lost." 13 So they gathered them up, and filled twelve baskets with broken pieces from the five barley loaves, which were left over by those who had eaten. 14 When therefore the people saw the sign which Jesus did, they said, "This is truly the prophet who comes into the world." 15 Jesus therefore, perceiving that they were about to come and take him by force to make him king, withdrew again to the mountain by himself.

1. Invite the Holy Spirit into this reading, asking the Author of Scripture to speak to you through His Word
2. Read today's passage as many times as you need, take your time
3. Write down (below) what the Lord is saying to you today
4. Live with this Word in your heart through the day

_____

_____

Sunday, August 4, 2024
EIGHTEENTH SUNDAY IN ORDINARY TIME

First Reading: Exodus 16: 2-4, 12-15

2 The whole congregation of the children of Israel murmured against Moses and against Aaron in the wilderness; 3 and the children of Israel said to them, "We wish that we had died by Yahweh's hand in the land of Egypt, when we sat by the meat pots, when we ate our fill of bread, for you have brought us out into this wilderness to kill this whole assembly with hunger."
4 Then Yahweh said to Moses, "Behold, I will rain bread from the sky for you, and the people shall go out and gather a day's portion every day, that I may test them, whether they will walk in my law or not.

12 "I have heard the murmurings of the children of Israel. Speak to them, saying, 'At evening you shall eat meat, and in the morning you shall be filled with bread. Then you will know that I am Yahweh your God.' "

13 In the evening, quail came up and covered the camp; and in the morning the dew lay around the camp. 14 When the dew that lay had gone, behold, on the surface of the wilderness was a small round thing, small as the frost on the ground. 15 When the children of Israel saw it, they said to one another, "What is it?" For they didn't know what it was. Moses said to them, "It is the bread which Yahweh has given you to eat.

Responsorial Psalm: Psalms 78: 3-4, 23-25, 54

3 which we have heard and known,
and our fathers have told us.
4 We will not hide them from their children,
telling to the generation to come the praises of Yahweh,
his strength, and his wondrous deeds that he has done.
23 Yet he commanded the skies above,
and opened the doors of heaven.
24 He rained down manna on them to eat,
and gave them food from the sky.
25 Man ate the bread of angels.
He sent them food to the full.
54 He brought them to the border of his sanctuary,
to this mountain, which his right hand had taken.

Second Reading: Ephesians 4: 17, 20-24

17 This I say therefore, and testify in the Lord, that you no longer walk as the rest of the Gentiles also walk, in the futility of their mind,
20 But you didn't learn Christ that way, 21 if indeed you heard him and were taught in him, even as truth is in Jesus: 22 that you put away, as concerning your former way of life, the old man that grows corrupt after the lusts of deceit, 23 and that you be renewed in the spirit of your mind, 24 and put on the new man, who in the likeness of God has been created in righteousness and holiness of truth.

Gospel: John 6: 24-35

24 When the multitude therefore saw that Jesus wasn't there, nor his disciples, they themselves got into the boats and came to Capernaum, seeking Jesus. 25 When they found him on the other side of the sea, they asked him, "Rabbi, when did you come here?"
26 Jesus answered them, "Most certainly I tell you, you seek me, not because you saw signs, but because you ate of the loaves and were filled. 27 Don't work for the food which perishes, but for the food which remains to eternal life, which the Son of Man will give to you. For God the Father has sealed him."
28 They said therefore to him, "What must we do, that we may work the works of God?"
29 Jesus answered them, "This is the work of God, that you believe in him whom he has sent."
30 They said therefore to him, "What then do you do for a sign, that we may see and believe you? What work do you do? 31 Our fathers ate the manna in the wilderness. As it is written, 'He gave them bread out of heaven† to eat.' "*
32 Jesus therefore said to them, "Most certainly, I tell you, it wasn't Moses who gave you the bread out of heaven, but my Father gives you the true bread out of heaven. 33 For the bread of God is that which comes down out of heaven and gives life to the world."
34 They said therefore to him, "Lord, always give us this bread."
35 Jesus said to them, "I am the bread of life. Whoever comes to me will not be hungry, and whoever believes in me will never be thirsty.

1. Invite the Holy Spirit into this reading, asking the Author of Scripture to speak to you through His Word
2. Read today's passage as many times as you need, take your time
3. Write down (below) what the Lord is saying to you today
4. Live with this Word in your heart through the day

_____

_____

Sunday, August 11, 2024
NINETEENTH SUNDAY IN ORDINARY TIME

First Reading: First Kings 19: 4-8

4 But he himself went a day's journey into the wilderness, and came and sat down under a juniper tree. Then he requested for himself that he might die, and said, "It is enough. Now, O Yahweh, take away my life; for I am not better than my fathers."
5 He lay down and slept under a juniper tree; and behold, an angel touched him, and said to him, "Arise and eat!"
6 He looked, and behold, there was at his head a cake baked on the coals, and a jar of water. He ate and drank, and lay down again. 7 Yahweh's angel came again the second time, and touched him, and said, "Arise and eat, because the journey is too great for you."
8 He arose, and ate and drank, and went in the strength of that food forty days and forty nights to Horeb, God's Mountain.

Responsorial Psalm: Psalms 34: 2-9

2 My soul shall boast in Yahweh.
The humble shall hear of it and be glad.
3 Oh magnify Yahweh with me.
Let's exalt his name together.
4 I sought Yahweh, and he answered me,
and delivered me from all my fears.
5 They looked to him, and were radiant.
Their faces shall never be covered with shame.
6 This poor man cried, and Yahweh heard him,
and saved him out of all his troubles.
7 Yahweh's angel encamps around those who fear him,
and delivers them.
8 Oh taste and see that Yahweh is good.
Blessed is the man who takes refuge in him.
9 Oh fear Yahweh, you his saints,
for there is no lack with those who fear him.

Second Reading: Ephesians 4: 30 – 5: 2

30 Don't grieve the Holy Spirit of God, in whom you were sealed for the day of redemption. 31 Let all bitterness, wrath, anger, outcry, and slander be put away from you, with all malice. 32 And be kind to one another, tender hearted, forgiving each other, just as God also in Christ forgave you.
1 Be therefore imitators of God, as beloved children. 2 Walk in love, even as Christ also loved us and gave himself up for us, an offering and a sacrifice to God for a sweet-smelling fragrance.

Gospel: John 6: 41-51

41 The Jews therefore murmured concerning him, because he said, "I am the bread which came down out of heaven." 42 They said, "Isn't this Jesus, the son of Joseph, whose father and mother we know? How then does he say, 'I have come down out of heaven'?"
43 Therefore Jesus answered them, "Don't murmur among yourselves. 44 No one can come to me unless the Father who sent me draws him; and I will raise him up in the last day. 45 It is written in the prophets, 'They will all be taught by God.' * Therefore everyone who hears from the Father and has learned, comes to me. 46 Not that anyone has seen the Father, except he who is from God. He has seen the Father. 47 Most certainly, I tell you, he who believes in me has eternal life. 48 I am the bread of life. 49 Your fathers ate the manna in the wilderness and they died. 50 This is the bread which comes down out of heaven, that anyone may eat of it and not die. 51 I am the living bread which came down out of heaven. If anyone eats of this bread, he will live forever. Yes, the bread which I will give for the life of the world is my flesh."

1. Invite the Holy Spirit into this reading, asking the Author of Scripture to speak to you through His Word
2. Read today's passage as many times as you need, take your time
3. Write down (below) what the Lord is saying to you today
4. Live with this Word in your heart through the day

_____

_____

Thursday, August 15, 2024
THE ASSUMPTION OF THE BLESSED VIRGIN MARY

First Reading: Revelation 11: 19a; 12: 1-6a, 10ab

19 God's temple that is in heaven was opened, and the ark of the Lord's covenant was seen in his temple.
1 A great sign was seen in heaven: a woman clothed with the sun, and the moon under her feet, and on her head a crown of twelve stars. 2 She was with child. She cried out in pain, laboring to give birth.
3 Another sign was seen in heaven. Behold, a great red dragon, having seven heads and ten horns, and on his heads seven crowns. 4 His tail drew one third of the stars of the sky, and threw them to the earth. The dragon stood before the woman who was about to give birth, so that when she gave birth he might devour her child. 5 She gave birth to a son, a male child, who is to rule all the nations with a rod of iron. Her child was caught up to God and to his throne. 6 The woman fled into the wilderness, where she has a place prepared by God, that there they may nourish her one thousand two hundred sixty days.
10 I heard a loud voice in heaven, saying, "Now the salvation, the power, and the Kingdom of our God, and the authority of his Christ has come; for the accuser of our brothers has been thrown down, who accuses them before our God day and night.

Responsorial Psalm: Psalms 45: 10, 11, 12, 16

10 Listen, daughter, consider, and turn your ear.
Forget your own people, and also your father's house.
11 So the king will desire your beauty,
honor him, for he is your lord.
12 The daughter of Tyre comes with a gift.
The rich among the people entreat your favor.
16 Your sons will take the place of your fathers.
You shall make them princes in all the earth.

Second Reading: First Corinthians 15: 20-27

20 But now Christ has been raised from the dead. He became the first fruit of those who are asleep. 21 For since death came by man, the resurrection of the dead also came

by man. 22 For as in Adam all die, so also in Christ all will be made alive. 23 But each in his own order: Christ the first fruits, then those who are Christ's at his coming. 24 Then the end comes, when he will deliver up the Kingdom to God the Father, when he will have abolished all rule and all authority and power. 25 For he must reign until he has put all his enemies under his feet. 26 The last enemy that will be abolished is death. 27 For, "He put all things in subjection under his feet."* But when he says, "All things are put in subjection", it is evident that he is excepted who subjected all things to him.

Gospel: Luke 1: 39-56

39 Mary arose in those days and went into the hill country with haste, into a city of Judah, 40 and entered into the house of Zacharias and greeted Elizabeth. 41 When Elizabeth heard Mary's greeting, the baby leaped in her womb; and Elizabeth was filled with the Holy Spirit. 42 She called out with a loud voice and said, "Blessed are you among women, and blessed is the fruit of your womb! 43 Why am I so favored, that the mother of my Lord should come to me? 44 For behold, when the voice of your greeting came into my ears, the baby leaped in my womb for joy! 45 Blessed is she who believed, for there will be a fulfillment of the things which have been spoken to her from the Lord!"

46 Mary said,
"My soul magnifies the Lord.
47 My spirit has rejoiced in God my Savior,
48 for he has looked at the humble state of his servant.
For behold, from now on, all generations will call me blessed.
49 For he who is mighty has done great things for me.
Holy is his name.
50 His mercy is for generations and generations on those who fear him.
51 He has shown strength with his arm.
He has scattered the proud in the imagination of their hearts.
52 He has put down princes from their thrones,
and has exalted the lowly.
53 He has filled the hungry with good things.
He has sent the rich away empty.
54 He has given help to Israel, his servant, that he might remember mercy,
55 as he spoke to our fathers,
to Abraham and his offspring§ forever."
56 Mary stayed with her about three months, and then returned to her house.

1. Invite the Holy Spirit into this reading, asking the Author of Scripture to speak to you through His Word
2. Read today's passage as many times as you need, take your time
3. Write down (below) what the Lord is saying to you today
4. Live with this Word in your heart through the day

_____

_____

Sunday, August 18, 2024
TWENTIETH SUNDAY IN ORDINARY TIME

First Reading: Proverbs 9: 1-6

1 Wisdom has built her house.
She has carved out her seven pillars.
2 She has prepared her meat.
She has mixed her wine.
She has also set her table.
3 She has sent out her maidens.
She cries from the highest places of the city:
4 "Whoever is simple, let him turn in here!"
As for him who is void of understanding, she says to him,
5 "Come, eat some of my bread,
Drink some of the wine which I have mixed!
6 Leave your simple ways, and live.
Walk in the way of understanding."

Responsorial Psalm: Psalms 34: 2-3, 10-15

2 My soul shall boast in Yahweh.
The humble shall hear of it and be glad.
3 Oh magnify Yahweh with me.

Let's exalt his name together.
10 The young lions do lack, and suffer hunger,
but those who seek Yahweh shall not lack any good thing.
11 Come, you children, listen to me.
I will teach you the fear of Yahweh.
12 Who is someone who desires life,
and loves many days, that he may see good?
13 Keep your tongue from evil,
and your lips from speaking lies.
14 Depart from evil, and do good.
Seek peace, and pursue it.
15 Yahweh's eyes are toward the righteous.
His ears listen to their cry.

Second Reading: Ephesians 5: 15-20

15 Therefore watch carefully how you walk, not as unwise, but as wise, 16 redeeming the time, because the days are evil. 17 Therefore, don't be foolish, but understand what the will of the Lord is. 18 Don't be drunken with wine, in which is dissipation, but be filled with the Spirit, 19 speaking to one another in psalms, hymns, and spiritual songs; singing and making melody in your heart to the Lord; 20 giving thanks always concerning all things in the name of our Lord Jesus Christ to God, even the Father;

Gospel: John 6: 51-58

51 I am the living bread which came down out of heaven. If anyone eats of this bread, he will live forever. Yes, the bread which I will give for the life of the world is my flesh."
52 The Jews therefore contended with one another, saying, "How can this man give us his flesh to eat?"
53 Jesus therefore said to them, "Most certainly I tell you, unless you eat the flesh of the Son of Man and drink his blood, you don't have life in yourselves. 54 He who eats my flesh and drinks my blood has eternal life, and I will raise him up at the last day. 55 For my flesh is food indeed, and my blood is drink indeed. 56 He who eats my flesh and drinks my blood lives in me, and I in him. 57 As the living Father sent me, and I live because of the Father, so he who feeds on me will also live because of me. 58 This

is the bread which came down out of heaven—not as our fathers ate the manna and died. He who eats this bread will live forever."

1. Invite the Holy Spirit into this reading, asking the Author of Scripture to speak to you through His Word
2. Read today's passage as many times as you need, take your time
3. Write down (below) what the Lord is saying to you today
4. Live with this Word in your heart through the day

_____

_____

Sunday, August 25, 2024
TWENTY-FIRST SUNDAY IN ORDINARY TIME

First Reading: Joshua 24: 1-2a, 15-17, 18b

1 Joshua gathered all the tribes of Israel to Shechem, and called for the elders of Israel, for their heads, for their judges, and for their officers; and they presented themselves before God. 2 Joshua said to all the people, "Yahweh, the God of Israel, says, 'Your fathers lived of old time beyond the River, even Terah, the father of Abraham, and the father of Nahor. They served other gods.
15 If it seems evil to you to serve Yahweh, choose today whom you will serve; whether the gods which your fathers served that were beyond the River, or the gods of the Amorites, in whose land you dwell; but as for me and my house, we will serve Yahweh." 16 The people answered, "Far be it from us that we should forsake Yahweh, to serve other gods; 17 for it is Yahweh our God who brought us and our fathers up out of the land of Egypt, from the house of bondage, and who did those great signs in our sight, and preserved us in all the way in which we went, and among all the peoples through the middle of whom we passed. 18 Yahweh drove out from before us all the peoples, even the Amorites who lived in the land. Therefore we also will serve Yahweh; for he is our God."

Responsorial Psalm: Psalms 34: 2-3, 16-22

2 My soul shall boast in Yahweh.
The humble shall hear of it and be glad.
3 Oh magnify Yahweh with me.
Let's exalt his name together.
16 Yahweh's face is against those who do evil,
to cut off their memory from the earth.
17 The righteous cry, and Yahweh hears,
and delivers them out of all their troubles.
18 Yahweh is near to those who have a broken heart,
and saves those who have a crushed spirit.
19 Many are the afflictions of the righteous,
but Yahweh delivers him out of them all.
20 He protects all of his bones.
Not one of them is broken.
21 Evil shall kill the wicked.
Those who hate the righteous shall be condemned.
22 Yahweh redeems the soul of his servants.
None of those who take refuge in him shall be condemned.

Second Reading: Ephesians 5: 21-32

21 subjecting yourselves to one another in the fear of Christ.
22 Wives, be subject to your own husbands, as to the Lord. 23 For the husband is the head of the wife, as Christ also is the head of the assembly, being himself the savior of the body. 24 But as the assembly is subject to Christ, so let the wives also be to their own husbands in everything.
25 Husbands, love your wives, even as Christ also loved the assembly and gave himself up for her, 26 that he might sanctify her, having cleansed her by the washing of water with the word, 27 that he might present the assembly to himself gloriously, not having spot or wrinkle or any such thing, but that she should be holy and without defect. 28 Even so husbands also ought to love their own wives as their own bodies. He who loves his own wife loves himself. 29 For no man ever hated his own flesh, but nourishes and cherishes it, even as the Lord also does the assembly, 30 because we are members of his body, of his flesh and bones. 31 "For this cause a man will leave his father and mother and will be joined to his wife. Then the two will become one flesh."* 32 This mystery is great, but I speak concerning Christ and the assembly.

Gospel: John 6: 60-69

60 Therefore many of his disciples, when they heard this, said, "This is a hard saying! Who can listen to it?"
61 But Jesus knowing in himself that his disciples murmured at this, said to them, "Does this cause you to stumble? 62 Then what if you would see the Son of Man ascending to where he was before? 63 It is the spirit who gives life. The flesh profits nothing. The words that I speak to you are spirit, and are life. 64 But there are some of you who don't believe." For Jesus knew from the beginning who they were who didn't believe, and who it was who would betray him. 65 He said, "For this cause I have said to you that no one can come to me, unless it is given to him by my Father."
66 At this, many of his disciples went back and walked no more with him. 67 Jesus said therefore to the twelve, "You don't also want to go away, do you?"
68 Simon Peter answered him, "Lord, to whom would we go? You have the words of eternal life. 69 We have come to believe and know that you are the Christ, the Son of the living God."

1. Invite the Holy Spirit into this reading, asking the Author of Scripture to speak to you through His Word
2. Read today's passage as many times as you need, take your time
3. Write down (below) what the Lord is saying to you today
4. Live with this Word in your heart through the day

_____

_____

Sunday, September 1, 2024
TWENTY-SECOND SUNDAY IN ORDINARY TIME

First Reading: Deuteronomy 4: 1-2, 6-8

1 Now, Israel, listen to the statutes and to the ordinances which I teach you, to do them, that you may live and go in and possess the land which Yahweh, the God of your fathers,

gives you. 2 You shall not add to the word which I command you, neither shall you take away from it, that you may keep the commandments of Yahweh your God which I command you.

6 Keep therefore and do them; for this is your wisdom and your understanding in the sight of the peoples who shall hear all these statutes and say, "Surely this great nation is a wise and understanding people." 7 For what great nation is there that has a god so near to them as Yahweh our God is whenever we call on him? 8 What great nation is there that has statutes and ordinances so righteous as all this law which I set before you today?

Responsorial Psalm: Psalms 15: 2-5

2 He who walks blamelessly and does what is right,
and speaks truth in his heart;
3 he who doesn't slander with his tongue,
nor does evil to his friend,
nor casts slurs against his fellow man;
4 in whose eyes a vile man is despised,
but who honors those who fear Yahweh;
he who keeps an oath even when it hurts, and doesn't change;
5 he who doesn't lend out his money for usury,
nor take a bribe against the innocent.

Second Reading: James 1: 17-18, 21b-22, 27

17 Every good gift and every perfect gift is from above, coming down from the Father of lights, with whom can be no variation nor turning shadow. 18 Of his own will he gave birth to us by the word of truth, that we should be a kind of first fruits of his creatures.
21 Therefore, putting away all filthiness and overflowing of wickedness, receive with humility the implanted word, which is able to save your souls.§
22 But be doers of the word, and not only hearers, deluding your own selves.
27 Pure religion and undefiled before our God and Father is this: to visit the fatherless and widows in their affliction, and to keep oneself unstained by the world.

Gospel: Mark 7: 1-8, 14-15, 21-23

1 Then the Pharisees and some of the scribes gathered together to him, having come from Jerusalem. 2 Now when they saw some of his disciples eating bread with defiled, that is unwashed, hands, they found fault. 3 (For the Pharisees and all the Jews don't eat unless they wash their hands and forearms, holding to the tradition of the elders. 4 They don't eat when they come from the marketplace unless they bathe themselves, and there are many other things which they have received to hold to: washings of cups, pitchers, bronze vessels, and couches.) 5 The Pharisees and the scribes asked him, "Why don't your disciples walk according to the tradition of the elders, but eat their bread with unwashed hands?"

6 He answered them, "Well did Isaiah prophesy of you hypocrites, as it is written,
'This people honors me with their lips,
but their heart is far from me.

7 They worship me in vain,
teaching as doctrines the commandments of men.'*

8 "For you set aside the commandment of God, and hold tightly to the tradition of men—the washing of pitchers and cups, and you do many other such things."

14 He called all the multitude to himself and said to them, "Hear me, all of you, and understand. 15 There is nothing from outside of the man that going into him can defile him; but the things which proceed out of the man are those that defile the man.

21 For from within, out of the hearts of men, proceed evil thoughts, adulteries, sexual sins, murders, thefts, 22 covetings, wickedness, deceit, lustful desires, an evil eye, blasphemy, pride, and foolishness. 23 All these evil things come from within and defile the man."

1. Invite the Holy Spirit into this reading, asking the Author of Scripture to speak to you through His Word
2. Read today's passage as many times as you need, take your time
3. Write down (below) what the Lord is saying to you today
4. Live with this Word in your heart through the day

_____

_____

Sunday, September 8, 2024
TWENTY-THIRD SUNDAY IN ORDINARY TIME

First Reading: Isaiah 35: 4-7a

4 Tell those who have a fearful heart, "Be strong!
Don't be afraid!
Behold, your God will come with vengeance, God's retribution.
He will come and save you.
5 Then the eyes of the blind will be opened,
and the ears of the deaf will be unstopped.
6 Then the lame man will leap like a deer,
and the tongue of the mute will sing;
for waters will break out in the wilderness,
and streams in the desert.
7 The burning sand will become a pool,
and the thirsty ground springs of water.

Responsorial Psalm: Psalms 146: 7-10

7 who executes justice for the oppressed;
who gives food to the hungry.
Yahweh frees the prisoners.
8 Yahweh opens the eyes of the blind.
Yahweh raises up those who are bowed down.
Yahweh loves the righteous.
9 Yahweh preserves the foreigners.
He upholds the fatherless and widow,
but he turns the way of the wicked upside down.
10 Yahweh will reign forever;
your God, O Zion, to all generations.
Praise Yah!

Second Reading: James 2: 1-5

1 My brothers, don't hold the faith of our glorious Lord Jesus Christ with partiality. 2 For if a man with a gold ring, in fine clothing, comes into your synagogue,† and a poor

man in filthy clothing also comes in, 3 and you pay special attention to him who wears the fine clothing and say, "Sit here in a good place;" and you tell the poor man, "Stand there," or "Sit by my footstool" 4 haven't you shown partiality among yourselves, and become judges with evil thoughts? 5 Listen, my beloved brothers. Didn't God choose those who are poor in this world to be rich in faith and heirs of the Kingdom which he promised to those who love him?

Gospel: Mark 7: 31-37

31 Again he departed from the borders of Tyre and Sidon, and came to the sea of Galilee through the middle of the region of Decapolis. 32 They brought to him one who was deaf and had an impediment in his speech. They begged him to lay his hand on him. 33 He took him aside from the multitude privately and put his fingers into his ears; and he spat and touched his tongue. 34 Looking up to heaven, he sighed, and said to him, "Ephphatha!" that is, "Be opened!" 35 Immediately his ears were opened, and the impediment of his tongue was released, and he spoke clearly. 36 He commanded them that they should tell no one, but the more he commanded them, so much the more widely they proclaimed it. 37 They were astonished beyond measure, saying, "He has done all things well. He makes even the deaf hear and the mute speak!"

1. Invite the Holy Spirit into this reading, asking the Author of Scripture to speak to you through His Word
2. Read today's passage as many times as you need, take your time
3. Write down (below) what the Lord is saying to you today
4. Live with this Word in your heart through the day

_____

_____

Sunday, September 15, 2024
TWENTY-FOURTH SUNDAY IN ORDINARY TIME

First Reading: Isaiah 50: 5-9a

5 The Lord Yahweh has opened my ear.
I was not rebellious.
I have not turned back.
6 I gave my back to those who beat me,
and my cheeks to those who plucked off the hair.
I didn't hide my face from shame and spitting.
7 For the Lord Yahweh will help me.
Therefore I have not been confounded.
Therefore I have set my face like a flint,
and I know that I won't be disappointed.
8 He who justifies me is near.
Who will bring charges against me?
Let us stand up together.
Who is my adversary?
Let him come near to me.
9 Behold, the Lord Yahweh will help me!
Who is he who will condemn me?
Behold, they will all grow old like a garment.
The moths will eat them up.

Responsorial Psalm: Psalms 116: 1-6, 8-9

1 I love Yahweh, because he listens to my voice,
and my cries for mercy.
2 Because he has turned his ear to me,
therefore I will call on him as long as I live.
3 The cords of death surrounded me,
the pains of Sheol† got a hold of me.
I found trouble and sorrow.
4 Then I called on Yahweh's name:
"Yahweh, I beg you, deliver my soul."
5 Yahweh is gracious and righteous.
Yes, our God is merciful.
6 Yahweh preserves the simple.
I was brought low, and he saved me.
8 For you have delivered my soul from death,
my eyes from tears,

and my feet from falling.
9 I will walk before Yahweh in the land of the living.

Second Reading: James 2: 14-18

14 What good is it, my brothers, if a man says he has faith, but has no works? Can faith save him? 15 And if a brother or sister is naked and in lack of daily food, 16 and one of you tells them, "Go in peace. Be warmed and filled;" yet you didn't give them the things the body needs, what good is it? 17 Even so faith, if it has no works, is dead in itself. 18 Yes, a man will say, "You have faith, and I have works." Show me your faith without works, and I will show you my faith by my works.

Gospel: Mark 8: 27-35

27 Jesus went out, with his disciples, into the villages of Caesarea Philippi. On the way he asked his disciples, "Who do men say that I am?"
28 They told him, "John the Baptizer, and others say Elijah, but others, one of the prophets."
29 He said to them, "But who do you say that I am?"
Peter answered, "You are the Christ."
30 He commanded them that they should tell no one about him. 31 He began to teach them that the Son of Man must suffer many things, and be rejected by the elders, the chief priests, and the scribes, and be killed, and after three days rise again. 32 He spoke to them openly. Peter took him and began to rebuke him. 33 But he, turning around and seeing his disciples, rebuked Peter, and said, "Get behind me, Satan! For you have in mind not the things of God, but the things of men."
34 He called the multitude to himself with his disciples and said to them, "Whoever wants to come after me, let him deny himself, and take up his cross, and follow me. 35 For whoever wants to save his life will lose it; and whoever will lose his life for my sake and the sake of the Good News will save it.

1. Invite the Holy Spirit into this reading, asking the Author of Scripture to speak to you through His Word
2. Read today's passage as many times as you need, take your time
3. Write down (below) what the Lord is saying to you today
4. Live with this Word in your heart through the day

Sunday, September 22, 2024
TWENTY-FIFTH SUNDAY IN ORDINARY TIME

First Reading: Wisdom 2: 12, 17-20

12 But let's lie in wait for the righteous man,
because he annoys us,
is contrary to our works,
reproaches us with sins against the law,
and charges us with sins against our training.
17 Let's see if his words are true.
Let's test what will happen at the end of his life.
18 For if the righteous man is God's son, he will uphold him,
and he will deliver him out of the hand of his adversaries.
19 Let's test him with insult and torture,
that we may find out how gentle he is,
and test his patience.
20 Let's condemn him to a shameful death,
for he will be protected, according to his words."

Responsorial Psalm: Psalms 54: 3-7

3 For strangers have risen up against me.
Violent men have sought after my soul.
They haven't set God before them.
4 Behold, God is my helper.
The Lord is the one who sustains my soul.
5 He will repay the evil to my enemies.
Destroy them in your truth.
6 With a free will offering, I will sacrifice to you.

I will give thanks to your name, Yahweh, for it is good.
7 For he has delivered me out of all trouble.
My eye has seen triumph over my enemies.

Second Reading: James 3: 16 – 4: 3

16 For where jealousy and selfish ambition are, there is confusion and every evil deed. 17 But the wisdom that is from above is first pure, then peaceful, gentle, reasonable, full of mercy and good fruits, without partiality, and without hypocrisy. 18 Now the fruit of righteousness is sown in peace by those who make peace.
1 Where do wars and fightings among you come from? Don't they come from your pleasures that war in your members? 2 You lust, and don't have. You murder and covet, and can't obtain. You fight and make war. You don't have, because you don't ask. 3 You ask, and don't receive, because you ask with wrong motives, so that you may spend it on your pleasures.

Gospel: Mark 9: 30-37

30 Then their eyes were opened. Jesus strictly commanded them, saying, "See that no one knows about this." 31 But they went out and spread abroad his fame in all that land.
32 As they went out, behold, a mute man who was demon possessed was brought to him. 33 When the demon was cast out, the mute man spoke. The multitudes marveled, saying, "Nothing like this has ever been seen in Israel!"
34 But the Pharisees said, "By the prince of the demons, he casts out demons."
35 Jesus went about all the cities and the villages, teaching in their synagogues and preaching the Good News of the Kingdom, and healing every disease and every sickness among the people. 36 But when he saw the multitudes, he was moved with compassion for them because they were harassed§ and scattered, like sheep without a shepherd. 37 Then he said to his disciples, "The harvest indeed is plentiful, but the laborers are few.

1. Invite the Holy Spirit into this reading, asking the Author of Scripture to speak to you through His Word
2. Read today's passage as many times as you need, take your time
3. Write down (below) what the Lord is saying to you today
4. Live with this Word in your heart through the day

Sunday, September 29, 2024
TWENTY-SIXTH SUNDAY IN ORDINARY TIME

First Reading: Numbers 11: 25-29

25 Yahweh came down in the cloud, and spoke to him, and took of the Spirit that was on him, and put it on the seventy elders. When the Spirit rested on them, they prophesied, but they did so no more. 26 But two men remained in the camp. The name of one was Eldad, and the name of the other Medad; and the Spirit rested on them. They were of those who were written, but had not gone out to the Tent; and they prophesied in the camp. 27 A young man ran, and told Moses, and said, "Eldad and Medad are prophesying in the camp!"
28 Joshua the son of Nun, the servant of Moses, one of his chosen men, answered, "My lord Moses, forbid them!"
29 Moses said to him, "Are you jealous for my sake? I wish that all Yahweh's people were prophets, that Yahweh would put his Spirit on them!"

Responsorial Psalm: Psalms 19: 8, 10, 12-13, 14

8 Yahweh's precepts are right, rejoicing the heart.
Yahweh's commandment is pure, enlightening the eyes.
10 They are more to be desired than gold, yes, than much fine gold,
sweeter also than honey and the extract of the honeycomb.
12 Who can discern his errors?
Forgive me from hidden errors.
13 Keep back your servant also from presumptuous sins.
Let them not have dominion over me.
Then I will be upright.
I will be blameless and innocent of great transgression.
14 Let the words of my mouth and the meditation of my heart

be acceptable in your sight,
Yahweh, my rock, and my redeemer.

Second Reading: James 5: 1-6

1 Come now, you rich, weep and howl for your miseries that are coming on you. 2 Your riches are corrupted and your garments are moth-eaten. 3 Your gold and your silver are corroded, and their corrosion will be for a testimony against you and will eat your flesh like fire. You have laid up your treasure in the last days. 4 Behold, the wages of the laborers who mowed your fields, which you have kept back by fraud, cry out; and the cries of those who reaped have entered into the ears of the Lord of Armies.† 5 You have lived in luxury on the earth, and taken your pleasure. You have nourished your hearts as in a day of slaughter. 6 You have condemned and you have murdered the righteous one. He doesn't resist you.

Gospel: Mark 9: 38-43, 45, 47-48

38 John said to him, "Teacher, we saw someone who doesn't follow us casting out demons in your name; and we forbade him, because he doesn't follow us."
39 But Jesus said, "Don't forbid him, for there is no one who will do a mighty work in my name and be able quickly to speak evil of me. 40 For whoever is not against us is on our side. 41 For whoever will give you a cup of water to drink in my name because you are Christ's, most certainly I tell you, he will in no way lose his reward.
42 "Whoever will cause one of these little ones who believe in me to stumble, it would be better for him if he were thrown into the sea with a millstone hung around his neck. 43 If your hand causes you to stumble, cut it off. It is better for you to enter into life maimed, rather than having your two hands to go into Gehenna, † into the unquenchable fire, 45 If your foot causes you to stumble, cut it off. It is better for you to enter into life lame, rather than having your two feet to be cast into Gehenna, § into the fire that will never be quenched—47 If your eye causes you to stumble, throw it out. It is better for you to enter into God's Kingdom with one eye, rather than having two eyes to be cast into the Gehenna‡ of fire, 48 'where their worm doesn't die, and the fire is not quenched.'

1. Invite the Holy Spirit into this reading, asking the Author of Scripture to speak to you through His Word

2. Read today's passage as many times as you need, take your time
3. Write down (below) what the Lord is saying to you today
4. Live with this Word in your heart through the day

_____

_____

Sunday, October 6, 2024
TWENTY-SEVENTH SUNDAY IN ORDINARY TIME

First Reading: Genesis 2: 18-24

18 Yahweh God said, "It is not good for the man to be alone. I will make him a helper comparable to§ him." 19 Out of the ground Yahweh God formed every animal of the field, and every bird of the sky, and brought them to the man to see what he would call them. Whatever the man called every living creature became its name. 20 The man gave names to all livestock, and to the birds of the sky, and to every animal of the field; but for man there was not found a helper comparable to him. 21 Yahweh God caused the man to fall into a deep sleep. As the man slept, he took one of his ribs, and closed up the flesh in its place. 22 Yahweh God made a woman from the rib which he had taken from the man, and brought her to the man. 23 The man said, "This is now bone of my bones, and flesh of my flesh. She will be called 'woman,' because she was taken out of Man." 24 Therefore a man will leave his father and his mother, and will join with his wife, and they will be one flesh.

Responsorial Psalm: Psalms 128: 1-6

1 Blessed is everyone who fears Yahweh,
who walks in his ways.
2 For you will eat the labor of your hands.
You will be happy, and it will be well with you.
3 Your wife will be as a fruitful vine in the innermost parts of your house,
your children like olive shoots around your table.
4 Behold, this is how the man who fears Yahweh is blessed.

5 May Yahweh bless you out of Zion,
and may you see the good of Jerusalem all the days of your life.
6 Yes, may you see your children's children.
Peace be upon Israel.

Second Reading: Hebrews 2: 9-11

9 But we see him who has been made a little lower than the angels, Jesus, because of the suffering of death crowned with glory and honor, that by the grace of God he should taste of death for everyone.
10 For it became him, for whom are all things and through whom are all things, in bringing many children to glory, to make the author of their salvation perfect through sufferings. 11 For both he who sanctifies and those who are sanctified are all from one, for which cause he is not ashamed to call them brothers,

Gospel: Mark 10: 2-16

2 Pharisees came to him testing him, and asked him, "Is it lawful for a man to divorce his wife?"
3 He answered, "What did Moses command you?"
4 They said, "Moses allowed a certificate of divorce to be written, and to divorce her."
5 But Jesus said to them, "For your hardness of heart, he wrote you this commandment. 6 But from the beginning of the creation, God made them male and female.* 7 For this cause a man will leave his father and mother, and will join to his wife, 8 and the two will become one flesh,* so that they are no longer two, but one flesh. 9 What therefore God has joined together, let no man separate."
10 In the house, his disciples asked him again about the same matter. 11 He said to them, "Whoever divorces his wife and marries another commits adultery against her. 12 If a woman herself divorces her husband and marries another, she commits adultery."
13 They were bringing to him little children, that he should touch them, but the disciples rebuked those who were bringing them. 14 But when Jesus saw it, he was moved with indignation and said to them, "Allow the little children to come to me! Don't forbid them, for God's Kingdom belongs to such as these. 15 Most certainly I tell you, whoever will not receive God's Kingdom like a little child, he will in no way enter into it." 16 He took them in his arms and blessed them, laying his hands on them.

1. Invite the Holy Spirit into this reading, asking the Author of Scripture to speak to you through His Word
2. Read today's passage as many times as you need, take your time
3. Write down (below) what the Lord is saying to you today
4. Live with this Word in your heart through the day

_____

_____

Sunday, October 13, 2024
TWENTY-EIGHTH SUNDAY IN ORDINARY TIME

First Reading: Wisdom 7: 7-11

7 For this cause I prayed, and understanding was given to me.
I asked, and a spirit of wisdom came to me.
8 I preferred her before sceptres and thrones.
I considered riches nothing in comparison to her.
9 Neither did I liken to her any priceless gem,
because all gold in her presence is a little sand,
and silver will be considered as clay before her.
10 I loved her more than health and beauty,
and I chose to have her rather than light,
because her bright shining is never laid to sleep.
11 All good things came to me with her,
and innumerable riches are in her hands.

Responsorial Psalm: Psalms 90: 12-17

12 So teach us to count our days,
that we may gain a heart of wisdom.
13 Relent, Yahweh!§
How long?

Have compassion on your servants!
14 Satisfy us in the morning with your loving kindness,
that we may rejoice and be glad all our days.
15 Make us glad for as many days as you have afflicted us,
for as many years as we have seen evil.
16 Let your work appear to your servants,
your glory to their children.
17 Let the favor of the Lord our God be on us.
Establish the work of our hands for us.
Yes, establish the work of our hands.

Second Reading: Hebrews 4: 12-13

12 For the word of God is living and active, and sharper than any two-edged sword, piercing even to the dividing of soul and spirit, of both joints and marrow, and is able to discern the thoughts and intentions of the heart. 13 There is no creature that is hidden from his sight, but all things are naked and laid open before the eyes of him to whom we must give an account.

Gospel: Mark 10: 17-30

17 As he was going out into the way, one ran to him, knelt before him, and asked him, "Good Teacher, what shall I do that I may inherit eternal life?"
18 Jesus said to him, "Why do you call me good? No one is good except one—God. 19 You know the commandments: 'Do not murder,' 'Do not commit adultery,' 'Do not steal,' 'Do not give false testimony,' 'Do not defraud,' 'Honor your father and mother.' "*
20 He said to him, "Teacher, I have observed all these things from my youth."
21 Jesus looking at him loved him, and said to him, "One thing you lack. Go, sell whatever you have and give to the poor, and you will have treasure in heaven; and come, follow me, taking up the cross."
22 But his face fell at that saying, and he went away sorrowful, for he was one who had great possessions.
23 Jesus looked around and said to his disciples, "How difficult it is for those who have riches to enter into God's Kingdom!"

24 The disciples were amazed at his words. But Jesus answered again, "Children, how hard it is for those who trust in riches to enter into God's Kingdom! 25 It is easier for a camel to go through a needle's eye than for a rich man to enter into God's Kingdom."
26 They were exceedingly astonished, saying to him, "Then who can be saved?"
27 Jesus, looking at them, said, "With men it is impossible, but not with God, for all things are possible with God."
28 Peter began to tell him, "Behold, we have left all and have followed you."
29 Jesus said, "Most certainly I tell you, there is no one who has left house, or brothers, or sisters, or father, or mother, or wife, or children, or land, for my sake, and for the sake of the Good News, 30 but he will receive one hundred times more now in this time: houses, brothers, sisters, mothers, children, and land, with persecutions; and in the age to come eternal life.

1. Invite the Holy Spirit into this reading, asking the Author of Scripture to speak to you through His Word
2. Read today's passage as many times as you need, take your time
3. Write down (below) what the Lord is saying to you today
4. Live with this Word in your heart through the day

Sunday, October 20, 2024
TWENTY-NINTH SUNDAY IN ORDINARY TIME

First Reading: Isaiah 53: 10-11

10 Yet it pleased Yahweh to bruise him.
He has caused him to suffer.
When you make his soul an offering for sin,
he will see his offspring.
He will prolong his days
and Yahweh's pleasure will prosper in his hand.
11 After the suffering of his soul,

he will see the light† and be satisfied.
My righteous servant will justify many by the knowledge of himself;
and he will bear their iniquities.

Responsorial Psalm: Psalms 33: 4-5, 18-20, 22

4 For Yahweh's word is right.
All his work is done in faithfulness.
5 He loves righteousness and justice.
The earth is full of the loving kindness of Yahweh.
18 Behold, Yahweh's eye is on those who fear him,
on those who hope in his loving kindness,
19 to deliver their soul from death,
to keep them alive in famine.
20 Our soul has waited for Yahweh.
He is our help and our shield.
22 Let your loving kindness be on us, Yahweh,
since we have hoped in you.

Second Reading: Hebrews 4: 14-16

14 Having then a great high priest who has passed through the heavens, Jesus, the Son of God, let's hold tightly to our confession. 15 For we don't have a high priest who can't be touched with the feeling of our infirmities, but one who has been in all points tempted like we are, yet without sin. 16 Let's therefore draw near with boldness to the throne of grace, that we may receive mercy and may find grace for help in time of need.

Gospel: Mark 10: 42-45

42 Jesus summoned them and said to them, "You know that they who are recognized as rulers over the nations lord it over them, and their great ones exercise authority over them. 43 But it shall not be so among you, but whoever wants to become great among you shall be your servant. 44 Whoever of you wants to become first among you shall be bondservant of all. 45 For the Son of Man also came not to be served but to serve, and to give his life as a ransom for many."

1. Invite the Holy Spirit into this reading, asking the Author of Scripture to speak to you through His Word
2. Read today's passage as many times as you need, take your time
3. Write down (below) what the Lord is saying to you today
4. Live with this Word in your heart through the day

_____

_____

Sunday, October 27, 2024
THIRTIETH SUNDAY IN ORDINARY TIME

First Reading: Jeremiah 31: 7-9

7 For Yahweh says,
"Sing with gladness for Jacob,
and shout for the chief of the nations.
Publish, praise, and say,
'Yahweh, save your people,
the remnant of Israel!'
8 Behold, I will bring them from the north country,
and gather them from the uttermost parts of the earth,
along with the blind and the lame,
the woman with child and her who travails with child together.
They will return as a great company.
9 They will come with weeping.
I will lead them with petitions.
I will cause them to walk by rivers of waters,
in a straight way in which they won't stumble;
for I am a father to Israel.
Ephraim is my firstborn.

Responsorial Psalm: Psalms 126: 1-6

1 When Yahweh brought back those who returned to Zion,
we were like those who dream.
2 Then our mouth was filled with laughter,
and our tongue with singing.
Then they said among the nations,
"Yahweh has done great things for them."
3 Yahweh has done great things for us,
and we are glad.
4 Restore our fortunes again, Yahweh,
like the streams in the Negev.
5 Those who sow in tears will reap in joy.
6 He who goes out weeping, carrying seed for sowing,
will certainly come again with joy, carrying his sheaves.

Second Reading: Hebrews 5: 1-6

1 For every high priest, being taken from among men, is appointed for men in things pertaining to God, that he may offer both gifts and sacrifices for sins. 2 The high priest can deal gently with those who are ignorant and going astray, because he himself is also surrounded with weakness. 3 Because of this, he must offer sacrifices for sins for the people, as well as for himself. 4 Nobody takes this honor on himself, but he is called by God, just like Aaron was. 5 So also Christ didn't glorify himself to be made a high priest, but it was he who said to him,
"You are my Son.
Today I have become your father."*
6 As he says also in another place,
"You are a priest forever,
after the order of Melchizedek."

Gospel: Mark 10: 46-52

46 They came to Jericho. As he went out from Jericho with his disciples and a great multitude, the son of Timaeus, Bartimaeus, a blind beggar, was sitting by the road. 47 When he heard that it was Jesus the Nazarene, he began to cry out and say, "Jesus, you

son of David, have mercy on me!" 48 Many rebuked him, that he should be quiet, but he cried out much more, "You son of David, have mercy on me!"
49 Jesus stood still and said, "Call him."
They called the blind man, saying to him, "Cheer up! Get up. He is calling you!"
50 He, casting away his cloak, sprang up, and came to Jesus.
51 Jesus asked him, "What do you want me to do for you?"
The blind man said to him, "Rabboni,† that I may see again."
52 Jesus said to him, "Go your way. Your faith has made you well." Immediately he received his sight and followed Jesus on the way.

1. Invite the Holy Spirit into this reading, asking the Author of Scripture to speak to you through His Word
2. Read today's passage as many times as you need, take your time
3. Write down (below) what the Lord is saying to you today
4. Live with this Word in your heart through the day

_____ _____

_____

Friday, November 1, 2024
ALL SAINTS

First Reading: Revelation 7: 2-4, 9-14

2 I saw another angel ascend from the sunrise, having the seal of the living God. He cried with a loud voice to the four angels to whom it was given to harm the earth and the sea, 3 saying, "Don't harm the earth, the sea, or the trees, until we have sealed the bondservants of our God on their foreheads!" 4 I heard the number of those who were sealed, one hundred forty-four thousand, sealed out of every tribe of the children of Israel

9 After these things I looked, and behold, a great multitude which no man could count, out of every nation and of all tribes, peoples, and languages, standing before the throne and before the Lamb, dressed in white robes, with palm branches in their hands. 10 They cried with a loud voice, saying, "Salvation be to our God, who sits on the throne, and to the Lamb!"

11 All the angels were standing around the throne, the elders, and the four living creatures; and they fell on their faces before his throne, and worshiped God, 12 saying, "Amen! Blessing, glory, wisdom, thanksgiving, honor, power, and might, be to our God forever and ever! Amen."
13 One of the elders answered, saying to me, "These who are arrayed in the white robes, who are they, and where did they come from?"
14 I told him, "My lord, you know."
He said to me, "These are those who came out of the great suffering.† They washed their robes and made them white in the Lamb's blood.

Responsorial Psalm: Psalms 24: 1b-6

1 The earth is Yahweh's, with its fullness;
the world, and those who dwell in it.
2 For he has founded it on the seas,
and established it on the floods.

3 Who may ascend to Yahweh's hill?
Who may stand in his holy place?
4 He who has clean hands and a pure heart;
who has not lifted up his soul to falsehood,
and has not sworn deceitfully.
5 He shall receive a blessing from Yahweh,
righteousness from the God of his salvation.
6 This is the generation of those who seek Him,
who seek your face—even Jacob.

Second Reading: First John 3: 1-3

1 See how great a love the Father has given to us, that we should be called children of God! For this cause the world doesn't know us, because it didn't know him. 2 Beloved, now we are children of God. It is not yet revealed what we will be; but we know that when he is revealed, we will be like him, for we will see him just as he is. 3 Everyone who has this hope set on him purifies himself, even as he is pure.

Gospel: Matthew 5: 1-12a

1 Seeing the multitudes, he went up onto the mountain. When he had sat down, his disciples came to him. 2 He opened his mouth and taught them, saying,
3 "Blessed are the poor in spirit,
for theirs is the Kingdom of Heaven.*
4 Blessed are those who mourn,
for they shall be comforted.*
5 Blessed are the gentle,
for they shall inherit the earth.†*
6 Blessed are those who hunger and thirst for righteousness,
for they shall be filled.
7 Blessed are the merciful,
for they shall obtain mercy.
8 Blessed are the pure in heart,
for they shall see God.
9 Blessed are the peacemakers,
for they shall be called children of God.
10 Blessed are those who have been persecuted for righteousness' sake,
for theirs is the Kingdom of Heaven.
11 "Blessed are you when people reproach you, persecute you, and say all kinds of evil against you falsely, for my sake. 12 Rejoice, and be exceedingly glad, for great is your reward in heaven. For that is how they persecuted the prophets who were before you.

1. Invite the Holy Spirit into this reading, asking the Author of Scripture to speak to you through His Word
2. Read today's passage as many times as you need, take your time
3. Write down (below) what the Lord is saying to you today
4. Live with this Word in your heart through the day

_____
_____

Sunday, November 3, 2024
THIRTY-FIRST SUNDAY IN ORDINARY TIME

First Reading: Deuteronomy 6: 2-6

2 that you might fear Yahweh your God, to keep all his statutes and his commandments, which I command you—you, your son, and your son's son, all the days of your life; and that your days may be prolonged. 3 Hear therefore, Israel, and observe to do it, that it may be well with you, and that you may increase mightily, as Yahweh, the God of your fathers, has promised to you, in a land flowing with milk and honey. 4 Hear, Israel: Yahweh is our God. Yahweh is one. 5 You shall love Yahweh your God with all your heart, with all your soul, and with all your might. 6 These words, which I command you today, shall be on your heart;

Responsorial Psalm: Psalms 18: 2-4, 47, 50

2 Yahweh is my rock, my fortress, and my deliverer;
my God, my rock, in whom I take refuge;
my shield, and the horn of my salvation, my high tower.
3 I call on Yahweh, who is worthy to be praised;
and I am saved from my enemies.
4 The cords of death surrounded me.
The floods of ungodliness made me afraid.
47 even the God who executes vengeance for me,
and subdues peoples under me.
50 He gives great deliverance to his king,
and shows loving kindness to his anointed,
to David and to his offspring,‡ forever more.

Second Reading: Hebrews 7: 23-28

23 Many, indeed, have been made priests, because they are hindered from continuing by death. 24 But he, because he lives forever, has his priesthood unchangeable. 25 Therefore he is also able to save to the uttermost those who draw near to God through him, seeing that he lives forever to make intercession for them.
26 For such a high priest was fitting for us: holy, guiltless, undefiled, separated from sinners, and made higher than the heavens; 27 who doesn't need, like those high priests, to offer up sacrifices daily, first for his own sins, and then for the sins of the

people. For he did this once for all, when he offered up himself. 28 For the law appoints men as high priests who have weakness, but the word of the oath, which came after the law, appoints a Son forever who has been perfected.

Gospel: Mark 12: 28b-34

28 One of the scribes came and heard them questioning together, and knowing that he had answered them well, asked him, "Which commandment is the greatest of all?"
29 Jesus answered, "The greatest is: 'Hear, Israel, the Lord our God, the Lord is one. 30 You shall love the Lord your God with all your heart, with all your soul, with all your mind, and with all your strength.'* This is the first commandment. 31 The second is like this: 'You shall love your neighbor as yourself.'* There is no other commandment greater than these."
32 The scribe said to him, "Truly, teacher, you have said well that he is one, and there is none other but he; 33 and to love him with all the heart, with all the understanding, all the soul, and with all the strength, and to love his neighbor as himself, is more important than all whole burnt offerings and sacrifices."
34 When Jesus saw that he answered wisely, he said to him, "You are not far from God's Kingdom."
No one dared ask him any question after that.

1. Invite the Holy Spirit into this reading, asking the Author of Scripture to speak to you through His Word
2. Read today's passage as many times as you need, take your time
3. Write down (below) what the Lord is saying to you today
4. Live with this Word in your heart through the day

_____
_____

Sunday, November 10, 2024
THIRTY-SECOND SUNDAY IN ORDINARY TIME

First Reading: First Kings 17: 10-16

10 So he arose and went to Zarephath; and when he came to the gate of the city, behold, a widow was there gathering sticks. He called to her and said, "Please get me a little water in a jar, that I may drink."

11 As she was going to get it, he called to her and said, "Please bring me a morsel of bread in your hand."

12 She said, "As Yahweh your God lives, I don't have anything baked, but only a handful of meal in a jar and a little oil in a jar. Behold, I am gathering two sticks, that I may go in and bake it for me and my son, that we may eat it, and die."

13 Elijah said to her, "Don't be afraid. Go and do as you have said; but make me a little cake from it first, and bring it out to me, and afterward make some for you and for your son. 14 For Yahweh, the God of Israel, says, 'The jar of meal will not run out, and the jar of oil will not fail, until the day that Yahweh sends rain on the earth.' "

15 She went and did according to the saying of Elijah; and she, he, and her household ate many days. 16 The jar of meal didn't run out and the jar of oil didn't fail, according to Yahweh's word, which he spoke by Elijah.

Responsorial Psalm: Psalms 146: 7-10

7 who executes justice for the oppressed;
who gives food to the hungry.
Yahweh frees the prisoners.
8 Yahweh opens the eyes of the blind.
Yahweh raises up those who are bowed down.
Yahweh loves the righteous.
9 Yahweh preserves the foreigners.
He upholds the fatherless and widow,
but he turns the way of the wicked upside down.
10 Yahweh will reign forever;
your God, O Zion, to all generations.
Praise Yah!

Second Reading: Hebrews 9: 24-28

24 For Christ hasn't entered into holy places made with hands, which are representations of the true, but into heaven itself, now to appear in the presence of God

for us; 25 nor yet that he should offer himself often, as the high priest enters into the holy place year by year with blood not his own, 26 or else he must have suffered often since the foundation of the world. But now once at the end of the ages, he has been revealed to put away sin by the sacrifice of himself. 27 Inasmuch as it is appointed for men to die once, and after this, judgment, 28 so Christ also, having been offered once to bear the sins of many, will appear a second time, not to deal with sin, but to save those who are eagerly waiting for him.

Gospel: Mark 12: 41-44

41 Jesus sat down opposite the treasury and saw how the multitude cast money into the treasury. Many who were rich cast in much. 42 A poor widow came and she cast in two small brass coins,† which equal a quadrans coin.‡ 43 He called his disciples to himself and said to them, "Most certainly I tell you, this poor widow gave more than all those who are giving into the treasury, 44 for they all gave out of their abundance, but she, out of her poverty, gave all that she had to live on."

1. Invite the Holy Spirit into this reading, asking the Author of Scripture to speak to you through His Word
2. Read today's passage as many times as you need, take your time
3. Write down (below) what the Lord is saying to you today
4. Live with this Word in your heart through the day

_____
_____

Sunday, November 17, 2024
THIRTY-THIRD SUNDAY IN ORDINARY TIME'

First Reading: Daniel 12: 1-3

1 "At that time Michael will stand up, the great prince who stands for the children of your people; and there will be a time of trouble, such as never was since there was a nation even to that same time. At that time your people will be delivered, everyone who

is found written in the book. 2 Many of those who sleep in the dust of the earth will awake, some to everlasting life, and some to shame and everlasting contempt. 3 Those who are wise will shine as the brightness of the expanse. Those who turn many to righteousness will shine as the stars forever and ever.

Responsorial Psalm: Psalms 16: 5, 8- 11

5 Yahweh assigned my portion and my cup.
You made my lot secure.
8 I have set Yahweh always before me.
Because he is at my right hand, I shall not be moved.
9 Therefore my heart is glad, and my tongue rejoices.
My body shall also dwell in safety.
10 For you will not leave my soul in Sheol,†
neither will you allow your holy one to see corruption.
11 You will show me the path of life.
In your presence is fullness of joy.
In your right hand there are pleasures forever more.

Second Reading: Hebrews 10: 11-14, 18

11 Every priest indeed stands day by day serving and offering often the same sacrifices, which can never take away sins, 12 but he, when he had offered one sacrifice for sins forever, sat down on the right hand of God, 13 from that time waiting until his enemies are made the footstool of his feet. 14 For by one offering he has perfected forever those who are being sanctified.
18 Now where remission of these is, there is no more offering for sin.

Gospel: Mark 13: 24-32

24 But in those days, after that oppression, the sun will be darkened, the moon will not give its light, 25 the stars will be falling from the sky, and the powers that are in the heavens will be shaken.* 26 Then they will see the Son of Man coming in clouds with great power and glory. 27 Then he will send out his angels, and will gather

together his chosen ones from the four winds, from the ends of the earth to the ends of the sky.

28 "Now from the fig tree, learn this parable. When the branch has now become tender and produces its leaves, you know that the summer is near; 29 even so you also, when you see these things coming to pass, know that it is near, at the doors. 30 Most certainly I say to you, this generation‡ will not pass away until all these things happen. 31 Heaven and earth will pass away, but my words will not pass away.

32 "But of that day or that hour no one knows—not even the angels in heaven, nor the Son, but only the Father.

1. Invite the Holy Spirit into this reading, asking the Author of Scripture to speak to you through His Word
2. Read today's passage as many times as you need, take your time
3. Write down (below) what the Lord is saying to you today
4. Live with this Word in your heart through the day

_____
_____

Sunday, November 24, 2024
OUR LORD JESUS CHRIST, KING OF THE UNIVERSE

First Reading: Daniel 7: 13-14

13 "I saw in the night visions, and behold, there came with the clouds of the sky one like a son of man, and he came even to the Ancient of Days, and they brought him near before him. 14 Dominion was given him, and glory, and a kingdom, that all the peoples, nations, and languages should serve him. His dominion is an everlasting dominion, which will not pass away, and his kingdom one that will not be destroyed.

Responsorial Psalm: Psalms 93: 1-2, 5

1 Yahweh reigns!
He is clothed with majesty!
Yahweh is armed with strength.
The world also is established.
It can't be moved.
2 Your throne is established from long ago.
You are from everlasting.
5 Your statutes stand firm.
Holiness adorns your house,
Yahweh, forever more.

Second Reading: Revelation 1: 5-8

5 and from Jesus Christ, the faithful witness, the firstborn of the dead, and the ruler of the kings of the earth. To him who loves us, and washed us from our sins by his blood—
6 and he made us to be a Kingdom, priests* to his God and Father—to him be the glory and the dominion forever and ever. Amen.
7 Behold,§ he is coming with the clouds, and every eye will see him, including those who pierced him. All the tribes of the earth will mourn over him. Even so, Amen.
8 "I am the Alpha and the Omega,†" says the Lord God,‡ "who is and who was and who is to come, the Almighty."

Gospel: John 18: 33b-37

33 Pilate therefore entered again into the Praetorium, called Jesus, and said to him, "Are you the King of the Jews?"
34 Jesus answered him, "Do you say this by yourself, or did others tell you about me?"
35 Pilate answered, "I'm not a Jew, am I? Your own nation and the chief priests delivered you to me. What have you done?"
36 Jesus answered, "My Kingdom is not of this world. If my Kingdom were of this world, then my servants would fight, that I wouldn't be delivered to the Jews. But now my Kingdom is not from here."
37 Pilate therefore said to him, "Are you a king then?"
Jesus answered, "You say that I am a king. For this reason I have been born, and for this reason I have come into the world, that I should testify to the truth. Everyone who is of the truth listens to my voice."

1. Invite the Holy Spirit into this reading, asking the Author of Scripture to speak to you through His Word
2. Read today's passage as many times as you need, take your time
3. Write down (below) what the Lord is saying to you today
4. Live with this Word in your heart through the day

_____

_____

Sunday, December 1, 2024
FIRST SUNDAY OF ADVENT

First Reading: Jeremiah 33: 14-16

14 "Behold, the days come," says Yahweh, "that I will perform that good word which I have spoken concerning the house of Israel and concerning the house of Judah.
15 "In those days and at that time,
I will cause a Branch of righteousness to grow up to David.
He will execute justice and righteousness in the land.
16 In those days Judah will be saved,
and Jerusalem will dwell safely.
This is the name by which she will be called:
Yahweh our righteousness."

Responsorial Psalm: Psalms 25: 4-5, 8-10, 14

4 Show me your ways, Yahweh.
Teach me your paths.
5 Guide me in your truth, and teach me,
for you are the God of my salvation.
I wait for you all day long.
8 Good and upright is Yahweh,
therefore he will instruct sinners in the way.

9 He will guide the humble in justice.
He will teach the humble his way.
10 All the paths of Yahweh are loving kindness and truth
to such as keep his covenant and his testimonies.
14 The friendship of Yahweh is with those who fear him.
He will show them his covenant.

Second Reading: First Thessalonians 3: 12 – 4: 2

12 May the Lord make you to increase and abound in love toward one another and toward all men, even as we also do toward you, 13 to the end he may establish your hearts blameless in holiness before our God and Father at the coming of our Lord Jesus with all his saints.
1 Finally then, brothers, we beg and exhort you in the Lord Jesus, that as you received from us how you ought to walk and to please God, that you abound more and more. 2 For you know what instructions we gave you through the Lord Jesus.

Gospel: Luke 21: 25-28, 34-36

25 "There will be signs in the sun, moon, and stars; and on the earth anxiety of nations, in perplexity for the roaring of the sea and the waves; 26 men fainting for fear and for expectation of the things which are coming on the world, for the powers of the heavens will be shaken. 27 Then they will see the Son of Man coming in a cloud with power and great glory. 28 But when these things begin to happen, look up and lift up your heads, because your redemption is near."
34 "So be careful, or your hearts will be loaded down with carousing, drunkenness, and cares of this life, and that day will come on you suddenly. 35 For it will come like a snare on all those who dwell on the surface of all the earth. 36 Therefore be watchful all the time, praying that you may be counted worthy to escape all these things that will happen, and to stand before the Son of Man."

1. Invite the Holy Spirit into this reading, asking the Author of Scripture to speak to you through His Word
2. Read today's passage as many times as you need, take your time
3. Write down (below) what the Lord is saying to you today
4. Live with this Word in your heart through the day

Sunday, December 8, 2024
SECOND SUNDAY OF ADVENT

First Reading: Baruch 5: 1-9

1 Take off the garment of your mourning and affliction, O Jerusalem, and put on forever the beauty of the glory from God. 2 Put on the robe of the righteousness from God. Set on your head a diadem of the glory of the Everlasting. 3 For God will show your splendor everywhere under heaven. 4 For your name will be called by God forever "Righteous Peace, Godly Glory".
5 Arise, O Jerusalem, and stand upon the height. Look around you toward the east and see your children gathered from the going down of the sun to its rising at the word of the Holy One, rejoicing that God has remembered them. 6 For they went from you on foot, being led away by their enemies, but God brings them in to you carried on high with glory, on a royal throne. 7 For God has appointed that every high mountain and the everlasting hills should be made low, and the valleys filled up to make the ground level, that Israel may go safely in the glory of God. 8 Moreover the woods and every sweet smelling tree have shaded Israel by the commandment of God. 9 For God will lead Israel with joy in the light of his glory with the mercy and righteousness that come from him.

Responsorial Psalm: Psalms 126: 1-6

1 When Yahweh brought back those who returned to Zion,
we were like those who dream.
2 Then our mouth was filled with laughter,
and our tongue with singing.
Then they said among the nations,
"Yahweh has done great things for them."
3 Yahweh has done great things for us,

and we are glad.
4 Restore our fortunes again, Yahweh,
like the streams in the Negev.
5 Those who sow in tears will reap in joy.
6 He who goes out weeping, carrying seed for sowing,
will certainly come again with joy, carrying his sheaves.

Second Reading: Philippians 1: 4-6, 8-11

4 always in every request of mine on behalf of you all, making my requests with joy, 5 for your partnership† in furtherance of the Good News from the first day until now; 6 being confident of this very thing, that he who began a good work in you will complete it until the day of Jesus Christ.
8 For God is my witness, how I long after all of you in the tender mercies of Christ Jesus.
9 This I pray, that your love may abound yet more and more in knowledge and all discernment, 10 so that you may approve the things that are excellent, that you may be sincere and without offense to the day of Christ, 11 being filled with the fruits of righteousness which are through Jesus Christ, to the glory and praise of God.

Gospel: Luke 3: 1-6

1 Now in the fifteenth year of the reign of Tiberius Caesar, Pontius Pilate being governor of Judea, and Herod being tetrarch of Galilee, and his brother Philip tetrarch of the region of Ituraea and Trachonitis, and Lysanias tetrarch of Abilene, 2 during the high priesthood of Annas and Caiaphas, the word of God came to John, the son of Zacharias, in the wilderness. 3 He came into all the region around the Jordan, preaching the baptism of repentance for remission of sins. 4 As it is written in the book of the words of Isaiah the prophet,
"The voice of one crying in the wilderness,
'Make ready the way of the Lord.
Make his paths straight.
5 Every valley will be filled.
Every mountain and hill will be brought low.
The crooked will become straight,
and the rough ways smooth.

6 All flesh will see God's salvation.' "

1. Invite the Holy Spirit into this reading, asking the Author of Scripture to speak to you through His Word
2. Read today's passage as many times as you need, take your time
3. Write down (below) what the Lord is saying to you today
4. Live with this Word in your heart through the day

_____

_____

Monday, December 9, 2024
THE IMMACULATE CONCEPTION OF THE BLESSED VIRGIN MARY
(Patronal Feastday of the United States of America)

First Reading: Genesis 3: 9-15, 20

9 Yahweh God called to the man, and said to him, "Where are you?"
10 The man said, "I heard your voice in the garden, and I was afraid, because I was naked; so I hid myself."
11 God said, "Who told you that you were naked? Have you eaten from the tree that I commanded you not to eat from?"
12 The man said, "The woman whom you gave to be with me, she gave me fruit from the tree, and I ate it."
13 Yahweh God said to the woman, "What have you done?"
The woman said, "The serpent deceived me, and I ate."
14 Yahweh God said to the serpent,
"Because you have done this,
you are cursed above all livestock,
and above every animal of the field.
You shall go on your belly
and you shall eat dust all the days of your life.
15 I will put hostility between you and the woman,
and between your offspring and her offspring.
He will bruise your head,

and you will bruise his heel."
20 The man called his wife Eve because she would be the mother of all the living.

Responsorial Psalm: Psalms 98: 1-4

1 Sing to Yahweh a new song,
for he has done marvelous things!
His right hand and his holy arm have worked salvation for him.
2 Yahweh has made known his salvation.
He has openly shown his righteousness in the sight of the nations.
3 He has remembered his loving kindness and his faithfulness toward the house of Israel.
All the ends of the earth have seen the salvation of our God.
4 Make a joyful noise to Yahweh, all the earth!
Burst out and sing for joy, yes, sing praises!

Second Reading: Ephesians 1: 3-6, 11-12

3 Blessed be the God and Father of our Lord Jesus Christ, who has blessed us with every spiritual blessing in the heavenly places in Christ, 4 even as he chose us in him before the foundation of the world, that we would be holy and without defect before him in love, 5 having predestined us for adoption as children through Jesus Christ to himself, according to the good pleasure of his desire, 6 to the praise of the glory of his grace, by which he freely gave us favor in the Beloved.
11 We were also assigned an inheritance in him, having been foreordained according to the purpose of him who does all things after the counsel of his will, 12 to the end that we should be to the praise of his glory, we who had before hoped in Christ.

Gospel: Luke 1: 26-38

26 Now in the sixth month, the angel Gabriel was sent from God to a city of Galilee named Nazareth, 27 to a virgin pledged to be married to a man whose name was Joseph, of David's house. The virgin's name was Mary. 28 Having come in, the angel said to her, "Rejoice, you highly favored one! The Lord is with you. Blessed are you among women!"

29 But when she saw him, she was greatly troubled at the saying, and considered what kind of salutation this might be. 30 The angel said to her, "Don't be afraid, Mary, for you have found favor with God. 31 Behold, you will conceive in your womb and give birth to a son, and shall name him 'Jesus.' 32 He will be great and will be called the Son of the Most High. The Lord God will give him the throne of his father David, 33 and he will reign over the house of Jacob forever. There will be no end to his Kingdom."
34 Mary said to the angel, "How can this be, seeing I am a virgin?"
35 The angel answered her, "The Holy Spirit will come on you, and the power of the Most High will overshadow you. Therefore also the holy one who is born from you will be called the Son of God. 36 Behold, Elizabeth your relative also has conceived a son in her old age; and this is the sixth month with her who was called barren. 37 For nothing spoken by God is impossible."‡
38 Mary said, "Behold, the servant of the Lord; let it be done to me according to your word."
Then the angel departed from her.

1. Invite the Holy Spirit into this reading, asking the Author of Scripture to speak to you through His Word
2. Read today's passage as many times as you need, take your time
3. Write down (below) what the Lord is saying to you today
4. Live with this Word in your heart through the day

Sunday, December 15, 2024
THIRD SUNDAY OF ADVENT

First Reading: Zephaniah 3: 14-18a

14 Sing, daughter of Zion! Shout, Israel! Be glad and rejoice with all your heart, daughter of Jerusalem. 15 Yahweh has taken away your judgments. He has thrown out your enemy. The King of Israel, Yahweh, is among you. You will not be afraid of evil any more. 16 In that day, it will be said to Jerusalem, "Don't be afraid, Zion. Don't let your hands be weak." 17 Yahweh, your God, is among you, a mighty one who will save.

He will rejoice over you with joy. He will calm you in his love. He will rejoice over you with singing. 18 I will remove those who grieve about the appointed feasts from you. They are a burden and a reproach to you.

Responsorial Psalm: Isaiah 12: 2-6

2 Behold, God is my salvation. I will trust, and will not be afraid; for Yah, Yahweh, is my strength and song; and he has become my salvation." 3 Therefore with joy you will draw water out of the wells of salvation. 4 In that day you will say, "Give thanks to Yahweh! Call on his name! Declare his doings among the peoples! Proclaim that his name is exalted! 5 Sing to Yahweh, for he has done excellent things! Let this be known in all the earth! 6 Cry aloud and shout, you inhabitant of Zion, for the Holy One of Israel is great among you!"

Second Reading: Philippians 4: 4-7

4 Rejoice in the Lord always! Again I will say, "Rejoice!" 5 Let your gentleness be known to all men. The Lord is at hand. 6 In nothing be anxious, but in everything, by prayer and petition with thanksgiving, let your requests be made known to God. 7 And the peace of God, which surpasses all understanding, will guard your hearts and your thoughts in Christ Jesus.

Gospel: Luke 3: 10-18

10 The multitudes asked him, "What then must we do?"
11 He answered them, "He who has two coats, let him give to him who has none. He who has food, let him do likewise."
12 Tax collectors also came to be baptized, and they said to him, "Teacher, what must we do?"
13 He said to them, "Collect no more than that which is appointed to you."
14 Soldiers also asked him, saying, "What about us? What must we do?"
He said to them, "Extort from no one by violence, neither accuse anyone wrongfully. Be content with your wages."
15 As the people were in expectation, and all men reasoned in their hearts concerning John, whether perhaps he was the Christ, 16 John answered them all, "I indeed baptize

you with water, but he comes who is mightier than I, the strap of whose sandals I am not worthy to loosen. He will baptize you in the Holy Spirit and fire. 17 His winnowing fan is in his hand, and he will thoroughly cleanse his threshing floor, and will gather the wheat into his barn; but he will burn up the chaff with unquenchable fire."
18 Then with many other exhortations he preached good news to the people

1. Invite the Holy Spirit into this reading, asking the Author of Scripture to speak to you through His Word
2. Read today's passage as many times as you need, take your time
3. Write down (below) what the Lord is saying to you today
4. Live with this Word in your heart through the day

_____

_____

Sunday, December 22, 2024
FOURTH SUNDAY OF ADVENT

First Reading: Micah 5: 1-4a

1 Now you shall gather yourself in troops,
daughter of troops.
He has laid siege against us.
They will strike the judge of Israel with a rod on the cheek.
2 But you, Bethlehem Ephrathah,
being small among the clans of Judah,
out of you one will come out to me who is to be ruler in Israel;
whose goings out are from of old, from ancient times.
3 Therefore he will abandon them until the time that she who is in labor gives birth.
Then the rest of his brothers will return to the children of Israel.
4 He shall stand, and shall shepherd in the strength of Yahweh,
in the majesty of the name of Yahweh his God.
They will live, for then he will be great to the ends of the earth.

Responsorial Psalm: Psalms 80: 2-3, 15-16, 18-19

2 Before Ephraim, Benjamin, and Manasseh, stir up your might!
Come to save us!
3 Turn us again, God.
Cause your face to shine,
and we will be saved.
15 the stock which your right hand planted,
the branch that you made strong for yourself.
16 It's burned with fire.
It's cut down.
They perish at your rebuke.
18 So we will not turn away from you.
Revive us, and we will call on your name.
19 Turn us again, Yahweh God of Armies.
Cause your face to shine, and we will be saved.

Second Reading: Hebrews 10: 5-10

5 Therefore when he comes into the world, he says,
"You didn't desire sacrifice and offering,
but you prepared a body for me.
6 You had no pleasure in whole burnt offerings and sacrifices for sin.
7 Then I said, 'Behold, I have come (in the scroll of the book it is written of me)
to do your will, O God.' "*
8 Previously saying, "Sacrifices and offerings and whole burnt offerings and sacrifices for sin you didn't desire, neither had pleasure in them" (those which are offered according to the law), 9 then he has said, "Behold, I have come to do your will." He takes away the first, that he may establish the second, 10 by which will we have been sanctified through the offering of the body of Jesus Christ once for all.

Gospel: Luke 1: 39-45

39 Mary arose in those days and went into the hill country with haste, into a city of Judah, 40 and entered into the house of Zacharias and greeted Elizabeth. 41 When Elizabeth heard Mary's greeting, the baby leaped in her womb; and Elizabeth was filled

with the Holy Spirit. 42 She called out with a loud voice and said, "Blessed are you among women, and blessed is the fruit of your womb! 43 Why am I so favored, that the mother of my Lord should come to me? 44 For behold, when the voice of your greeting came into my ears, the baby leaped in my womb for joy! 45 Blessed is she who believed, for there will be a fulfillment of the things which have been spoken to her from the Lord!"

1. Invite the Holy Spirit into this reading, asking the Author of Scripture to speak to you through His Word
2. Read today's passage as many times as you need, take your time
3. Write down (below) what the Lord is saying to you today
4. Live with this Word in your heart through the day

_____

_____

Tuesday, December 24, 2024

First Reading: Second Samuel 7: 1-5, 8b-12, 14a, 16

1 When the king lived in his house, and Yahweh had given him rest from all his enemies all around, 2 the king said to Nathan the prophet, "See now, I dwell in a house of cedar, but God's ark dwells within curtains."
3 Nathan said to the king, "Go, do all that is in your heart, for Yahweh is with you."
4 That same night, Yahweh's word came to Nathan, saying, 5 "Go and tell my servant David, 'Yahweh says, "Should you build me a house for me to dwell in?
8 Now therefore tell my servant David this: 'Yahweh of Armies says, "I took you from the sheep pen, from following the sheep, to be prince over my people, over Israel. 9 I have been with you wherever you went, and have cut off all your enemies from before you. I will make you a great name, like the name of the great ones who are in the earth. 10 I will appoint a place for my people Israel, and will plant them, that they may dwell in their own place and be moved no more. The children of wickedness will not afflict them any more, as at the first, 11 and as from the day that I commanded judges to be over my people Israel. I will cause you to rest from all your enemies. Moreover Yahweh tells you that Yahweh will make you a house. 12 When your days are fulfilled and you

sleep with your fathers, I will set up your offspring after you, who will proceed out of your body, and I will establish his kingdom.
14a I will be his father, and he will be my son. 15 but my loving kindness will not depart from him, as I took it from Saul, whom I put away before you. 16 Your house and your kingdom will be made sure forever before you. Your throne will be established forever."
'

Responsorial Psalm: Psalms 89: 2-5, 27 and 29

2 I indeed declare, "Love stands firm forever.
You established the heavens.
Your faithfulness is in them."
3 "I have made a covenant with my chosen one,
I have sworn to David, my servant,
4 'I will establish your offspring forever,
and build up your throne to all generations.' "
5 The heavens will praise your wonders, Yahweh,
your faithfulness also in the assembly of the holy ones.
27 I will also appoint him my firstborn,
the highest of the kings of the earth.
29 I will also make his offspring endure forever,
and his throne as the days of heaven.

Gospel: Luke 1: 67-79

67 His father Zacharias was filled with the Holy Spirit, and prophesied, saying,
68 "Blessed be the Lord, the God of Israel,
for he has visited and redeemed his people;
69 and has raised up a horn of salvation for us in the house of his servant David
70 (as he spoke by the mouth of his holy prophets who have been from of old),
71 salvation from our enemies and from the hand of all who hate us;
72 to show mercy toward our fathers,
to remember his holy covenant,
73 the oath which he swore to Abraham our father,
74 to grant to us that we, being delivered out of the hand of our enemies,
should serve him without fear,

75 in holiness and righteousness before him all the days of our life.
76 And you, child, will be called a prophet of the Most High;
for you will go before the face of the Lord to prepare his ways,
77 to give knowledge of salvation to his people by the remission of their sins,
78 because of the tender mercy of our God,
by which the dawn from on high will visit us,
79 to shine on those who sit in darkness and the shadow of death;
to guide our feet into the way of peace."

1. Invite the Holy Spirit into this reading, asking the Author of Scripture to speak to you through His Word
2. Read today's passage as many times as you need, take your time
3. Write down (below) what the Lord is saying to you today
4. Live with this Word in your heart through the day

_____

_____

Wednesday, December 25, 2024
THE NATIVITY OF THE LORD (Christmas)

First Reading: Isaiah 52: 7-10

7 How beautiful on the mountains are the feet of him who brings good news,
who publishes peace,
who brings good news,
who proclaims salvation,
who says to Zion, "Your God reigns!"
8 Your watchmen lift up their voice.
Together they sing;
for they shall see eye to eye when Yahweh returns to Zion.
9 Break out into joy!
Sing together, you waste places of Jerusalem;
for Yahweh has comforted his people.
He has redeemed Jerusalem.

10 Yahweh has made his holy arm bare in the eyes of all the nations.
All the ends of the earth have seen the salvation of our God.

Responsorial Psalm: Psalms 98: 1-6

1 Sing to Yahweh a new song,
for he has done marvelous things!
His right hand and his holy arm have worked salvation for him.
2 Yahweh has made known his salvation.
He has openly shown his righteousness in the sight of the nations.
3 He has remembered his loving kindness and his faithfulness toward the house of Israel.
All the ends of the earth have seen the salvation of our God.
4 Make a joyful noise to Yahweh, all the earth!
Burst out and sing for joy, yes, sing praises!
5 Sing praises to Yahweh with the harp,
with the harp and the voice of melody.
6 With trumpets and sound of the ram's horn,
make a joyful noise before the King, Yahweh.

Second Reading: Hebrews 1: 1-6

1 God, having in the past spoken to the fathers through the prophets at many times and in various ways, 2 has at the end of these days spoken to us by his Son, whom he appointed heir of all things, through whom also he made the worlds. 3 His Son is the radiance of his glory, the very image of his substance, and upholding all things by the word of his power, who, when he had by himself purified us of our sins, sat down on the right hand of the Majesty on high, 4 having become as much better than the angels as the more excellent name he has inherited is better than theirs. 5 For to which of the angels did he say at any time,
"You are my Son.
Today I have become your father?"*
and again,
"I will be to him a Father,
and he will be to me a Son?"*

6 When he again brings in the firstborn into the world he says, "Let all the angels of God worship him."

Gospel: John 1: 1-18

1 In the beginning was the Word, and the Word was with God, and the Word was God. 2 The same was in the beginning with God. 3 All things were made through him. Without him, nothing was made that has been made. 4 In him was life, and the life was the light of men. 5 The light shines in the darkness, and the darkness hasn't overcome† it.
6 There came a man sent from God, whose name was John. 7 The same came as a witness, that he might testify about the light, that all might believe through him. 8 He was not the light, but was sent that he might testify about the light. 9 The true light that enlightens everyone was coming into the world.
10 He was in the world, and the world was made through him, and the world didn't recognize him. 11 He came to his own, and those who were his own didn't receive him. 12 But as many as received him, to them he gave the right to become God's children, to those who believe in his name: 13 who were born, not of blood, nor of the will of the flesh, nor of the will of man, but of God.
14 The Word became flesh and lived among us. We saw his glory, such glory as of the only born‡ Son of the Father, full of grace and truth. 15 John testified about him. He cried out, saying, "This was he of whom I said, 'He who comes after me has surpassed me, for he was before me.' " 16 From his fullness we all received grace upon grace. 17 For the law was given through Moses. Grace and truth were realized through Jesus Christ.§ 18 No one has seen God at any time. The only born† Son,‡ who is in the bosom of the Father, has declared him.

1. Invite the Holy Spirit into this reading, asking the Author of Scripture to speak to you through His Word
2. Read today's passage as many times as you need, take your time
3. Write down (below) what the Lord is saying to you today
4. Live with this Word in your heart through the day

_____

_____

Sunday, December 29, 2024
THE HOLY FAMILY OF JESUS, MARY AND JOSEPH

First Reading: First Samuel 1: 20-22, 24-28

20 When the time had come, Hannah conceived, and bore a son; and she named him Samuel,§ saying, "Because I have asked him of Yahweh."
21 The man Elkanah, and all his house, went up to offer to Yahweh the yearly sacrifice and his vow. 22 But Hannah didn't go up, for she said to her husband, "Not until the child is weaned; then I will bring him, that he may appear before Yahweh, and stay there forever."
24 When she had weaned him, she took him up with her, with three bulls, and one ephah† of meal, and a container of wine, and brought him to Yahweh's house in Shiloh. The child was young. 25 They killed the bull, and brought the child to Eli. 26 She said, "Oh, my lord, as your soul lives, my lord, I am the woman who stood by you here, praying to Yahweh. 27 I prayed for this child, and Yahweh has given me my petition which I asked of him. 28 Therefore I have also given him to Yahweh. As long as he lives he is given to Yahweh." He worshiped Yahweh there.

Responsorial Psalm: Psalms 84: 2-3, 5-6, 9-10

2 My soul longs, and even faints for the courts of Yahweh.
My heart and my flesh cry out for the living God.
3 Yes, the sparrow has found a home,
and the swallow a nest for herself, where she may have her young,
near your altars, Yahweh of Armies, my King, and my God.
5 Blessed are those whose strength is in you,
who have set their hearts on a pilgrimage.
6 Passing through the valley of Weeping, they make it a place of springs.
Yes, the autumn rain covers it with blessings.
9 Behold, God our shield,
look at the face of your anointed.
10 For a day in your courts is better than a thousand.
I would rather be a doorkeeper in the house of my God,
than to dwell in the tents of wickedness.

Second Reading: First John 3: 1-2, 21-24

1 See how great a love the Father has given to us, that we should be called children of God! For this cause the world doesn't know us, because it didn't know him. 2 Beloved, now we are children of God. It is not yet revealed what we will be; but we know that when he is revealed, we will be like him, for we will see him just as he is.
21 Beloved, if our hearts don't condemn us, we have boldness toward God; 22 so whatever we ask, we receive from him, because we keep his commandments and do the things that are pleasing in his sight. 23 This is his commandment, that we should believe in the name of his Son, Jesus Christ, and love one another, even as he commanded. 24 He who keeps his commandments remains in him, and he in him. By this we know that he remains in us, by the Spirit which he gave us.

Gospel: Luke 2: 41-52

41 His parents went every year to Jerusalem at the feast of the Passover. 42 When he was twelve years old, they went up to Jerusalem according to the custom of the feast; 43 and when they had fulfilled the days, as they were returning, the boy Jesus stayed behind in Jerusalem. Joseph and his mother didn't know it, 44 but supposing him to be in the company, they went a day's journey; and they looked for him among their relatives and acquaintances. 45 When they didn't find him, they returned to Jerusalem, looking for him. 46 After three days they found him in the temple, sitting in the middle of the teachers, both listening to them and asking them questions. 47 All who heard him were amazed at his understanding and his answers. 48 When they saw him, they were astonished; and his mother said to him, "Son, why have you treated us this way? Behold, your father and I were anxiously looking for you."
49 He said to them, "Why were you looking for me? Didn't you know that I must be in my Father's house?" 50 They didn't understand the saying which he spoke to them. 51 And he went down with them and came to Nazareth. He was subject to them, and his mother kept all these sayings in her heart. 52 And Jesus increased in wisdom and stature, and in favor with God and men.

1. Invite the Holy Spirit into this reading, asking the Author of Scripture to speak to you through His Word
2. Read today's passage as many times as you need, take your time
3. Write down (below) what the Lord is saying to you today

4. Live with this Word in your heart through the day

_____
_____

NOTES

Printed in Great Britain
by Amazon